W9-BWC-728

γ

MODERN WORLD NATIONS

Sweden

Edward Patrick Hogan
South Dakota State University

and

Joan Marie Hogan

Series Consulting Editor
Charles F. Gritzner
South Dakota State University

CHELSEA HOUSE
PUBLISHERS
An imprint of Infobase Publishing

Frontispiece: Flag of Sweden

Cover: Midsummer's Day celebrations are held at the end of June when the vegetation is lush and sunshine lasts almost all day long. A garland-covered maypole is raised in the afternoon and the people circle around it dancing and singing.

Sweden

Copyright © 2006 by Infobase Publishing

Chelsea House
An imprint of Infobase Publishing
132 West 31st Street
New York NY 10001

Library of Congress Cataloging-in-Publication Data

Hogan, Edward Patrick, 1939–
    Sweden/Edward Patrick Hogan and Joan Marie Hogan.
        p. cm.—(Modern world nations)
    Includes bibliographical references and index.
    ISBN 0-7910-8799-9 (hard cover)
    1. Sweden—Juvenile literature. I. Hogan, Joan Marie. II. Title. III. Series.
DL609.H58 2005
948.5—dc22   2005026499

Chelsea House books are available at special discounts when purchased in bulk quantities for businesses, associations, institutions, or sales promotions. Please call our Special Sales Department in New York at (212) 967-8800 or (800) 322-8755.

You can find Chelsea House on the World Wide Web at http://www.chelseahouse.com

Text design by Takeshi Takahashi
Cover design by Keith Trego

Printed in the United States of America

Bang 21C 10 9 8 7 6 5 4 3 2 1

This book is printed on acid-free paper.

All links, web addresses, and Internet search terms were checked and verified to be correct at the time of publication. Because of the dynamic nature of the web, some addresses and links may have changed since publication and may no longer be valid.

Table of Contents

Sweden

Introducing
Sweden

S weden has developed a worldwide reputation for excellence. It is renowned for producing high-quality steels, superior motor vehicles, and distinctive furniture. Sweden is also recognized for its pleasing cuisine and is especially famous for introducing the world to the smorgasbord (smörgåsbord). The smorgasbord has gained almost universal recognition as a distinct type of meal, featuring numerous food choices. The smorgasbord originated in Sweden, but its fame spread across Scandinavia, then to Great Britain, on to the United States, and today to the rest of the world. Americans refer to this type of meal more commonly as a buffet, and the restaurants featuring it offer informal service.

Historically, the Scandinavians toasted each other with *aquavit*— "the water of life," a potent potato-based drink. Several hundred years ago snacks were added to the toasting celebration. By the nineteenth century, the smorgasbord had evolved into a feast.

Then and now, a smorgasbord begins with a clean plate and a selection of herring enjoyed with aquavit, which is followed by cold dishes, hot dishes, baked goods, and desserts. Family and friends were invited to the smorgasbord and often brought other food dishes to the table. Normally, a family would host only two or three such celebrations a year. In turn, a family was invited to participate in other families' smorgasbords as well.

The smorgasbord is both a collection of local foods reflecting the culture's preparation traditions and a unique celebration of Swedish cuisine. In a very real sense, the geographic journey you are about to begin is similar to a smorgasbord. Your journey will examine the physical environment and the cultural heritage of the Kingdom of Sweden. Just as a smorgasbord is a celebration utilizing a variety of foods, this intellectual meal comprises a variety of physical and cultural factors that when combined result in a geographic celebration of Sweden.

Each chapter of the text will begin by introducing you to particular food dishes in the order that they are found in the smorgasbord. By the last chapter, you will be able to understand and visualize the entire Swedish feast. In a similar manner, each chapter will introduce you to the physical and cultural elements that build on each other to provide you with an understanding of Sweden.

The Kingdom of Sweden is located on the Scandinavian Peninsula, near the northwestern limit of the continent of Europe. Sweden's boundary with Norway to the north and west, its longest land border, extends 1,006 miles (1,619 kilometers). Sweden's other continental border, with Finland, in the northeast, extends almost 382 miles (614 kilometers). Water surrounds the rest of the country. The coastline extends 1,999 miles (3,218 kilometers) from where Sweden's land abuts Finland to the point where it borders Norway in the southwest. The Swedish islands of Öland and Gotland are located off the southeastern coast, in the Baltic Sea.

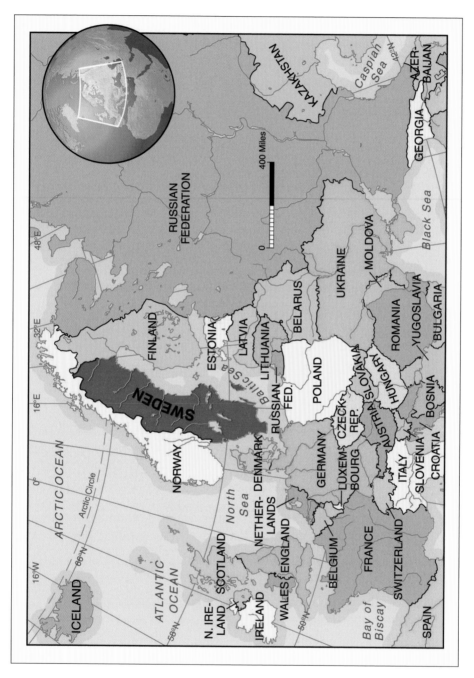

Sweden is located in northern Europe, bordering on the Baltic Sea, Gulf of Bothnia, and Kattegat and Skagerrak straits, and situated between Norway on the north and west, Denmark on the south, and Finland on the north and east.

Sweden is located between 55°20' and 69°04' north latitude and between 10°58' and 24°10' east longitude. The country has an area of 173,732 square miles (449,964 square kilometers), making it slightly larger than the state of California or the state of Montana. Sweden's shape is somewhat similar to an elongated kidney bean. Its greatest length extends from north to south approximately 1,000 miles (1,610 kilometers). Its greatest breadth from west to east is about 250 miles (400 kilometers).

Sweden is a beautiful country. Shaped by ice, its mountains, valleys, plains, and coastline provide fantastic vistas. Much of the landscape is covered by large expanses of lush forests, which are home to a variety of birds and animals. The country possesses valuable mineral resources. It is blessed with fertile agricultural lands in the south and numerous types of sea life in its bay and in its island-studded coastal zone.

All of Sweden enjoys four contrasting seasons. Northern Sweden is a "land of the midnight sun." During much of July and August, daylight can last up to 24 hours, whereas during the winter months of December and January, the only sunshine seen is a few hours of twilight.

Sweden has had an exciting history. Swedish Vikings played key roles in the exploration and development of modern-day Russia and Ukraine. In concert with other Scandinavian Vikings, they dominated the then-known world. Following the Viking decline, Sweden was governed first by strong kings and more recently by a strong parliament with a ceremonial monarchy. Sweden now has a democratic constitutional monarchy with an extensive system of social welfare programs. Today, Sweden has also attained one of the world's highest standards of living.

Christianity reached Sweden more than 1,000 years ago. In the sixteenth century, King Gustav I Vasa led the Protestant Reformation in Sweden, replacing Catholicism with the Evangelical Lutheran Church, and establishing it as the state church. Today, although the vast majority of its people claim

Sweden is a land of majestic beauty: much of the northern two-thirds of the country is made up of vast forests and mountains. Along the southern coast, ports such as the one pictured here serve as centers of trade, where goods are imported and exported.

membership in that church, few attend services. Thus, Sweden can be described as one of the more secular nations in the world.

The population of Sweden exceeds nine million citizens. From 1820 until about 1940, the country experienced substantial immigration to the United States. Now, it receives equally significant emigration from Europe and other world areas. Sweden has also become increasingly urbanized. Housing programs have played a key role in that process. Today, 83.3 percent of the population lives in urban areas.

Sweden plays an important role in world trade. Its traditional economies have provided a solid economic foundation for a new and diversified manufacturing economy. The country has also established a large service economy that supports the needs of its welfare system, government, and individual and corporate businesses.

Sweden is an important world social force. Although a neutral nation with a welfare society, Sweden does not shirk its responsibilities to the European or world communities. As an active leader in the United Nations, Sweden embraced the UN Declaration on Human Rights in 1948. Through its commitment to equality for all, the government provides welfare services and programming for all citizens, including the indigenous Sami and recently immigrated people. Sweden has also become an active diplomatic force in world politics. Native sons Alfred Nobel and Dag Hammarskjöld have led major efforts to facilitate world peace.

2

Physical Geography

W e begin our meal by approaching the smorgasbord table, picking up a large plate, and selecting small portions of several dishes for our first course. Generally, this includes six or seven herring dishes, such as sweet pickled herring, matjes herring with sour cream (pickled young herring), herring marinated in mustard, böckling (smoked herring), raw Baltic herring, Baltic herring pickled in vinegar, and fried pickled herring in onions. This course may also include herring and beetroot salad, sun-eyes (boiled egg yokes), roe (fish eggs), boiled potatoes, onions, bread, butter, and cheese. A small glass of aquavit or beer may complete this course. This is similar to what Americans call appetizers or *hors d'oeuvres*. These foods and drinks are served at the beginning of the meal to stimulate your taste buds, as you progress to the other dinner courses.

Similarly, a geographic journey begins with understanding the physical environment of the place in which the adventure is set. Like the first course of a smorgasbord, the physical environment comprises the various distinct phenomena, each of which is capable of being enjoyed on its own. Like appetizers, though, when sampled together, these geographic phenomena awaken one's tastes and senses to further pleasures. Thus, we begin our journey by focusing on Sweden's physical geography.

The terrain of Sweden is often described as flat. In the United States, a similar description is used for South Dakota, although the state contains deep river valleys, beautiful hills, the Badlands, and the mountainous Black Hills. The same is true of Sweden. Whereas there are certainly areas of flat land, there is far more hill country, as well as ice-scoured coasts and spectacular mountains.

Several processes have worked to create and shape Sweden's topography (land features). The folding and faulting of the earth's crust have created mountains, and volcanism has also contributed to the process. Glacial ice and flowing water have eroded and sculpted land in one place and deposited its debris elsewhere. Mass movements, such as landslides and earth flows, have also helped to shape the land.

GLACIERS

Glaciers have played the most important role in shaping Sweden's contemporary landscape. During the Pleistocene epoch (Ice Age), the Scandinavian Ice Sheet (continental glacier) dominated northern Europe, reaching to the British Isles and into much of Russia. At its greatest extent, this massive sheet of ice was approximately one mile (more than 1,750 meters) thick and spread outward in all directions. The volume of this mass compressed the land below it. About 12,000 years ago, the Ice Age ended and the Scandinavian Ice Sheet retreated. As the ice melted, the land slowly began to rise in elevation, a process that continues today.

As the Scandinavian Ice Sheet expanded, it attacked the landscape of Sweden like a gigantic bulldozer. The ice scoured land in one place and deposited rock and other earth materials in another. As the ice sheet melted and retreated, it left a variety of depositional and fluvial (flowing water) landforms. These include eskers, drumlins, glacial lakes, and moraines. In Sweden, the most significant of these is the esker. Eskers are depositional landforms created as sand and gravel were deposited on the floor of tunnels formed within melting glaciers. As the ice retreated, the esker continued building backwards for miles. One notable esker near Uppsala is more than 100 miles (160 kilometers) long. Another glacial landform found in Sweden, the drumlin, is a smoothly rounded hill shaped like an overturned teaspoon; drumlins are normally found grouped across the landscape. Sweden also is home to almost 100,000 lakes. The vast majority of these lakes exist in glacial-scoured depressions that filled with melted glacial water.

In the mountains of Sweden, as in neighboring Norway, alpine (high-elevation) glaciation has and continues to shape the terrain. Norway has more than 1,700 active alpine glaciers, but Sweden has only about 250. Like the ice sheets, alpine glaciers bulldoze the rock and soil from one place and deposit it in another, while carving deeply into the land below. Alpine glaciers flow downward from mountaintops, carving U-shaped valleys, hanging troughs, arêtes (ridges), and Matterhorn peaks. As they retreat, they leave behind tarns (mountain lakes), hanging waterfalls, and glacial deposits of sand and gravel. Alpine glaciers also leave other features, including abrasion marks in exposed bedrock, rock debris deposited as stratified drift or till, and hills and moraines (piles of debris).

In both Sweden's mountain and coastal areas, glaciers have carved cavernous U-shaped valleys. In the mountains, streams cascade as scenic waterfalls from "hanging valleys" into the glacially scoured valley below. In coastal areas, these deep U-shaped valleys have filled with water from rising sea levels to create spectacular fjords.

There are nearly 100,000 lakes in Sweden, including Lake Glan, which is located along the southeastern coast, near the town of Norrkoping. Nine percent of Sweden's surface area is covered by lakes, more than half of which occupy an area of more than two acres.

TERRAIN

Sweden and Norway share the Scandinavian Peninsula. The dominant physical feature of the peninsula is the Kjølen Mountain Range, which extends from north to south and reaches its highest elevations on the peninsula's western margin. In Sweden, this range dominates the lands along and east of its border with Norway. Geologically, the Kjølen Mountains are part of the massive Caledonian Mountains. This ancient range extends southwestward from the Scandinavia Peninsula, slips beneath the North Sea, and emerges once again in Ireland. It was created some 600 million years ago by tectonic activity that included faulting and folding. In that process, enormous blocks of earth were uplifted and thrust over previously existing lands. Over time, the physiographic (earth's surface) forces of erosion and rejuvenation have also played important roles in shaping the contemporary landscape of Sweden.

Geologically, Sweden is a land of ancient rocks; it contains some of the oldest geologic material in the world. Extensive areas of Sweden are composed of igneous and metamorphic bedrocks of granite and gneiss. The pressures of faulting and folding have changed some of these granite rocks into metamorphic gneiss. Other areas are composed of fine-grained extruded volcanic rock known as schist. These areas possess important mineral deposits, most notably, iron ore. Sedimentary zones of sandstone, limestone, shale, and clays also cover extensive areas of the south and narrow coastal lands.

Physiographic Regions

Today, Sweden's physical landscape consists of three distinct physiographic regions. The largest of these is Norrland (Northland). It covers the northern 60 percent of the country. Sveland (the Land of the Swedes) is located directly south of Norrland and extends from the border with Norway to the Baltic Sea. The third physiographic region is Götaland (Land of the Goths), Sweden's southernmost lands, which are bounded by the North Sea's Kattegatt Straight to the west and the Baltic Sea to the east.

Norrland (Northland) is a land of physiographic diversity. In the western part, it is noted for the fjäll, a region of mountains and rough hills cut by steep valleys. East of the fjäll, the landscape decreases in elevation and becomes a plains environment, with river valleys that extend to the eastern coastal plain and the sea. In this region, isolated hills or low mountains known as monadnocks (300 to 600 feet, or 100–200 meters, high) can also be found. The terrain of the coastal plains along the Gulf of Bothnia varies. In southern Norrland, the plain of the High Coast contains fjords, U-shaped estuaries with rugged 600- to

The terrain of Sweden is often described as flat, although it contains deep river valleys, beautiful hills, and mountains. Glaciers have played the most important role in shaping Sweden's contemporary landscape. During the Ice Age, a massive sheet of ice compressed the land and as that ice melted, the land began to slowly rise in elevation.

900-foot (200- to 300-meter) cliffs. Along Norrland's northern coast, the plains are delimited by off-shore islands and beaches. Swift down-cutting streams with rapids and waterfalls flow in deep river valleys, from northwest to southeast. Eskers are also found in this region. Elevation varies from sea level in the east to over 6,500 feet (2,000 meters) in the west. The western Kjølen Mountains contain the highest point in Sweden, Mt. Kebnekaise, which rises to 6,926 feet (2,111 meters).

More than one-third of Norrland lies north of the Arctic Circle (66 1/2° north latitude). This portion of the region is known as the Sápmi (Saamiland, or Lappland), because it is home to the Sami (Lapp) people. Norrland also contains several of Sweden's national parks and UNESCO World Heritage sites.

The second physiographic region, Sveland, lies to the south. It is a land of faint relief that has been uplifted, eroded, and otherwise altered over time. Elevation ranges from sea level to 650 feet (200 meters). Sveland crosses Sweden from the shore of the Baltic Sea to roughly the country's boundary with Norway. The landscape is dominated by three separate glacial clay-covered plains created by faulted downfolds, separated by higher remnants of plateaus and hills. Glaciation also is responsible for the presence of thousands of lakes in this region. Sveland has a low or level landscape dominated by remnants of a plateau in the west that slopes downward into undulating hills and a coastal plain in the east. At its eastern edge, Sveland is defined by archipelagos (island chains) comprising thousands of small islands.

Götaland, the third and southernmost physiographic region, encompasses a complex landscape. Elevation ranges from sea level to 1,240 feet (378 meters). It includes the southern highlands of Småland and the low fertile plain of Skåne. The highlands of Småland parallel Sveland, extending across the country from west to east. On the west coast, they are delineated by beaches, islands, and fjords and on the eastern Baltic Sea coast by *fjards*. A fjard is a glacial U-shaped inlet of the sea created just like a fjord but surrounded by rocky lowlands rather than cliffs. Between the coasts, the highlands are dissected by stream valleys and dotted with lakes. Lake Vattern, the third-largest lake in Europe, is located in this portion of Götaland.

South of this subregion, the landscape changes into the Southern Smäland Plain, which spans Sweden from coast to coast. The plain is very level, with an average height of about 500 feet (150 meters) above sea level. The third subregion of Götaland is known as Skåne. This landscape is a modified plain that has been faulted. As a result, it is composed of a series of horst (upthrust) ridges extending 160–750 feet (200–225 meters) above sea level. The surface is glaciated and contains glacial features similar to the rest of Sweden. At its extreme southern end, Götaland is defined by a faulted coastline with few inlets and a hammerhead-shaped spit (sandbar) notorious for causing navigation problems.

The two large islands of Gotland and Öland are located in the Baltic Sea, off Sweden's southeast coast. These elongated islands parallel the coast and are part of the country's territory. Both islands are built on limestone bedrock and are composed of flat plateau-like surfaces that slope eastward. Öland, 85 miles (136 kilometers) long and 4 to 10 miles (6 to 16 kilometers) wide, is located less than 3 miles (5.5 kilometers) off the mainland. The larger Gotland, 77 miles (125 kilometers) long and up to 31 miles (50 kilometers) wide, is located 56 miles (90 kilometers) from the mainland.

WEATHER AND CLIMATE

Weather is the day-by-day condition of the atmosphere, whereas climate is weather averaged over a lengthy period of time. Latitude and location are the primary influences on Sweden's weather and climate. The country spans some 14° of latitude, the northern portion of which extends toward the north pole from the Arctic Circle. This north-south distance of about 1,000 miles (1,610 kilometers) causes the weather and climate in Sweden to vary from area to area. If compared to Alaska, Sweden's latitudinal span would extend from Kodiak Island in extreme southern Alaska, northward to the Arctic Ocean. Even though Alaska and Sweden share similar latitudes, their populations vary greatly. Sweden is home to more than 9 million people. Alaska, although about four times the size of Sweden, has a population of just over 600,000.

Why is the population of the two countries so different? Location helps to answer this question. Sweden is located in northwestern Europe surrounded by well-established nations with large populations, whereas Alaska is remote and isolated from the major North American population base. The Arctic Ocean provides little protection for Alaska, but Sweden is protected by Norway, its mountainous neighbor to its north and west. Climatically, both Norway and Sweden benefit from the Gulf Stream and North Atlantic Drift. This broad "river" of water originates in the tropical Atlantic and transports warm equatorial water into the northeast Atlantic. As the prevailing westerly winds blow across this warmed water and onto the Scandinavian Peninsula, they bathe the region with much warmer air than one would expect at these northerly latitudes. As a result, Sweden's climate is much less severe than that of other lands to the north and east.

Climate in Sweden can be categorized into three distinct zones or types. Southern Sweden (Götaland) has a Marine West Coast climate. The westerlies blowing in from the North Sea moderate the temperatures of this southern 20 percent of the nation all year long. As a result, summers and winters are both milder than in its continental climate counterparts to the north. Precipitation falls throughout the year, although there is slightly more in the summer.

Central Sweden and southern Norrland have a Humid Continental Long Winter climate. Geographically, this climate type encircles the earth in the Arctic region. In North America, it extends from Alaska to Labrador. In Sweden, this continental climate is one of extremes. Summer rainfall in Sweden is affected by neighboring mountainous Norway. As the eastward-blowing winds cross the mountains, the now drier air flows down into Sweden. Winters are long and very cold, with periods of below-zero temperatures. Snow can cover this region's landscape for much of the year. Seasonal temperature variations are also greater in this climate than in other parts of Sweden. Central Sweden and southern Norrland lie in a zone of storms. Blizzards and severe snow storms occur during the long winter and even in fall or spring. In the summer, surprisingly, this region can and has experienced the effects of powerful thunderstorms and even tornadoes.

The northern Norrland region has a Polar Tundra climate. This climatic type covers the northern fringes of Europe, Asia, and North America. The Polar Tundra climate is defined by long cold winters and very short summers. The region's annual precipitation is light, with the heaviest amounts occurring during the short summer season.

It has been said, "In Sweden, summer is the warmest day of the year." Truthfully, Sweden does have four seasons, although the length and strength of each season varies significantly by location.

THE MIDNIGHT SUN

Because of its geographic position, Sweden, like neighboring Norway and Finland, is often referred to as "the Land of the Midnight Sun." This "eternal sunshine" lasts for almost two months each summer. This is because the rotating earth is tilted on its axis 23 1/2 degrees, as it revolves around the sun. At the summer solstice, it reaches a point in its orbit where the Northern Hemisphere is tilted toward the sun as it rotates, resulting in 24 hours of daylight. Conversely, the opposite is true during the December winter solstice, when the northern hemisphere of the revolving earth is tilted away from the sun, thus exposing points in the Arctic to long periods of continuous darkness.

Although Sweden is called the "Land of the Midnight Sun," it is also a land of considerable cloudiness. This is especially true in Sweden's western fjäll, where as many as 200 cloudy days occur each year. The west coast of Gotland is the foggiest area of Sweden, with fog occurring as often as one out of every four days.

PLANT AND ANIMAL LIFE

About 10,000 years ago, Sweden was emerging from the Scandinavian Ice Age. The massive ice sheets that covered the landscape were retreating, and the exposed lands were blanketed with mosses and lichens. By 8,000 years ago, the region's climate had changed to allow the spread of vegetation across the landscape. In higher elevations, the fjäll and moors were covered with mosses, lichens, and flowering plants. Below the tree line and southward, northern forests of pine and birch covered the landscape. In the south and in lower elevations, lowlands oak and beech forests dominated.

Some 5,000 years ago, the climate began to cool again. With the cooling, came a change in vegetation. Norway spruce entered Sweden and in time became the country's dominant tree. During this time, pine, birch, aspen, and oak were pushed to the north and west. Oak was replaced by birch and aspen as the predominant deciduous tree species. Today, needle-leaved conifers dominate the natural vegetation of Sweden, comprising about 85 percent of the trees. The Norway spruce is the dominant type, with pine ranking second in importance. Birch is the most common deciduous tree.

Other forms of plant life in Sweden vary by climate and place. More than 2,000 species of flowering plants grow here. Wood anemones carpet the forests, water lilies dot the surface of many lakes, and orchids thrive in swampy highland areas. Peat bogs are another notable form of plant life in Sweden. Peat lands result from lakes becoming overgrown by various forms of plant life that do not decompose. As a result, lake bottoms

Sweden boasts the highest density of moose per square mile in the world—more than 250,000 roam the country's wilderness. The moose, also called elk in Sweden and other European countries, is the largest member of the deer family and often weighs more than 1,000 pounds.

become clogged with layers of organic debris that eventually become peat.

Sweden's fauna (animal life) has been influenced by climate and humankind. The forests are home to a large variety of animal life. Particularly important are the moose and deer. In Sweden, the moose (also called elk, but not to be confused with the North American animal with the same name) is the largest wild animal. With some 250,000 moose, Sweden has the world's highest density of this majestic animal. The deer population is also quite large. The roe, red, and fallow deer all inhabit Sweden, with roe being the most common. Reindeer are also present in large numbers in Norrland's Sápmi region, but they are a domesticated, rather than wild, animal.

Other important species of animal life are predators that include the wolf, brown bear, lynx, wolverine, red fox, and polar fox. Sweden's vast forests are also home to lemmings, hares, rabbits, hedgehogs, squirrels, rats, and beavers, which thrive in the forest environment.

Lemmings, small migratory rodents 6 inches (15 centimeters) in length, exhibit an interesting life cycle. Every 11 or 12 years they experience a huge population explosion. When this happens, millions of lemming fall off cliffs, drown in the lakes or sea, or are eaten by predators as they migrate across the land. These periods are called "the lemming years." As the lemmings migrate, other animals and birds feast on their weak and their young. Amazingly, during these periods, snowy owls instinctively know of the event and fly thousands of miles across Eurasia's tundra region to dine on Sweden's lemmings.

Sweden is blessed with a wide variety of birds, including mountain and black grouse, ptarmigan, sea eagles, and several species of owls. Eagles, owls, buzzards, and hawks are the main birds of prey, although several of the species are now threatened.

Sea life, an important part of Sweden's fauna, varies from lakes to rivers to the sea. Freshwater river and lake species include pike, perch, trout, and whiting. Salmon are found in both the rivers and seas. In the sea, mackerel, herring, and cod are the most common fish species. Lobster, shrimp, and other shellfish also thrive in the coastal environment. In addition, Sweden's coastal areas are home to thousands of seals.

WATER FEATURES

Sweden is a landscape dominated by water. It is dotted by almost 100,000 lakes and drained by numerous rivers and streams. The country is bordered by scenic coastal fjords and archipelagos and surrounded on three sides by the sea.

Nine percent of Sweden's surface area is covered by lakes, more than half of which occupy an area of more than two acres (.8 hectares). Four lakes, Vänern, Vättern, Mälaren, and Hjälmaren, are so large that they make up about one-quarter of Sweden's total lake surface area. Further, Lake Vänern is the third-largest lake in all of Europe. The water quality of these lakes varies greatly, from humus-filled bog lakes to crystal clear tarns (mountain lakes).

Sweden is also a land of swift-flowing streams, draining primarily from the western fjäll to the Gulf of Bothnia, the Baltic, or North Sea. Glacial debris and hydropower projects have formed several large finger-like (elongated) lakes and reservoirs along the course of the rivers. Water flow in Sweden varies greatly by the season. The greatest volume normally results from spring and summer snowmelt and rainfall. The principal rivers of Sweden from north to south are the Torneälven, Luleälven, Umeälven, Indalsälven, Ljusnan, Dalälven, and Klarälven. Sweden's rivers are valuable resources of hydroelectric power. They are also important tourism and recreation resources. In addition, the combined surface waters from lakes and rivers provide more than one-half of the nation's drinking water.

MINERAL RESOURCES

Sweden harbors abundant nonmetallic mineral resources. These include limestone for cement, various building stones such as granite and slate, crushed stone, sand, and gravel for construction. The most important metallic mineral is iron ore. In fact, Sweden has the world's largest and richest deposits of this metal. Other major metallic minerals found in Sweden include zinc, lead, copper, gold, and silver. Uranium is also mined.

Except for some peat extraction, mineral fuels such as coal and petroleum are lacking. No commercially feasible deposits of either mineral fuel have been found in Sweden. Instead, the country relies on its abundant access to water and its use for hydroelectric power. Fortunately, the landscape is ideal for development of this resource.

SUMMARY

Sweden is a uniquely beautiful land. Its terrain varies from spectacular glaciated landscapes in the north to broad lowland plains in the south. Despite its northern position, the country is considerably warmer than might be expected. Climatic conditions vary from a quite mild and pleasant Temperate Marine climate in the south to a cold Polar Tundra climate in the far north. Soils suitable for farming are widespread in the south, where temperatures are milder and the growing season longer.

Today, pine forests cover more than 60 percent of the landscape, and another 10 percent of the country is covered with lakes or wetlands. Woodlands provide a splendid natural habitat for wildlife, including reindeer, moose, deer, and smaller animals. Coastal areas, numerous rivers, and thousands of lakes provide excellent environments for various species of sea life. Sweden is blessed with extensive deposits of metallic and nonmetallic materials. Historically, iron ore deposits have been the backbone of Sweden's industrial economy. Although poor in mineral fuels, uranium has enabled Sweden to develop nuclear power. With this understanding of Sweden's physical geography, we can now begin examining the cultural landscape and the impact of the people on the land.

3

Historical Geography

The second course of the smorgasbord consists of dishes of cold seafood, Sweden's basic source of protein. The traditional dishes served during this course are marinated salmon, smoked salmon, poached salmon, roe, shrimp, oysters, mussels, and sauces. Just as the proteins in seafood are essential building blocks for humans, the knowledge of Sweden's history is an essential building block to understand the country's historical geography.

Whereas historians study history by focusing on timelines, geographers study human history by focusing on cultural landscapes. The cultural landscape is the visible imprint of human activities on Earth's surface. These imprints are reflected in numerous cultural features, including monuments, buildings, roads, and communities. Present-day cultural landscapes are imprinted by previous inhabitants. In this chapter, we will note how, when, and where Swedes changed their cultural landscapes as we reveal layers of these previous cultural imprints.

EARLIEST OCCUPANTS

Approximately 12,000 years ago, the vast glacial ice sheets that had covered Eurasia and North America began retreating. At that point, parts of Scandinavia's freshly glaciated landscape became habitable. It took another 6,000 years, however, before the entire peninsula emerged from beneath its blanket of glacial ice. The new landscape was rugged and sloped downward from the mountainous west to the coastal plains on the east. In the south, the landscape was lower in elevation and flatter. The weather in this new land was harsh. Over time, as the climate warmed to a point that plant life could be sustained, the landscape quickly became home for animals and humans.

With the end of the Ice Age, the first Stone Age human occupants, journeying from Central Asia, entered southern Sweden. Very likely they were the ancestors of the Sami (Lapps), who still occupy areas of northern Norway, Sweden, and Finland.

These early occupants were hunters and fishers, who migrated seasonally across the land with all their possessions. Evidence of their presence can still be found on the landscape in cairns (stone monuments) and petroglyphs (rock carvings). Their stone tools are also displayed in several museums across Sweden. One significant example of their imprint on the cultural landscape is at Skegriedösen, the site of a massive Stone Age burial mound unique to southern and western Sweden.

The next arrivals came from present-day Denmark. Germanic in origin, they settled in western and southern Sweden and survived as fishermen. In addition to cairns, their spatial distribution and imprints on the landscape have been verified though studies of midden piles (trash heaps). Scientists trace the movements, settlements, life styles, and artifacts of ancient peoples by studying these waste piles and their contents.

Cairns (stone monuments) such as these on Oland Island in the Baltic Sea serve as reminders of Sweden's ancient past. Stone Age (6000 B.C. to 4000 B.C.) inhabitants of Sweden set up these stone structures to serve as boundary markers, memorials, or burial sites.

Presence of these early humans is also reflected in agriculture. Some 5,000 years ago, agriculture was introduced into Denmark and southern regions of Sweden and Norway. The Germanic peoples adopted tools, as well as crops and livestock practices, from neighboring cultures. About the same time, Scandinavia experienced a climatic shift. The Swedes had to further modify their practices and shift their emphasis to crops and livestock that would do well in a cooler environment.

Bronze Age Peoples

The Bronze Age reached southern Scandinavia about 1800 B.C., gradually spread northward, and lasted until around 500 B.C.

These peoples' lives changed dramatically during this age. In the south, agricultural settlements increased in number. A chieftain society with weaponry developed. Wooden instruments were gradually replaced with Bronze Age tools and weapons obtained in trade from the south. The emergence of solar wheels indicates that the people very likely became sun worshipers. These Bronze Age people continued to imprint the landscape with cairns, burial mounds, and petroglyphs.

Tanum, a UNESCO World Heritage Site on Sweden's western coast, contains numerous rock carvings depicting Bronze Age life. This extensive 3,000-year-old site includes many symbols for daily life, battles, hunting, fishing, and the afterlife.

The Iron Age

The Iron Age reached Sweden about 500 B.C. and lasted for more than 1,000 years. Iron tools and weapons entered Sweden from Germanic areas to the south. Cultural evidence also indicates trade with the Roman Empire. Evidence includes glass items, jewelry, new tools, coins, and Latin lettering. At the same time, Roman and Greek maps began to reflect the presence of Thule, an island north of Denmark. In A.D. 98, Tacitus, a Roman historian, wrote *Germania*, in which he refers to the "Sviones" as a powerful people, with weapons and ships.

During the Iron Age, the use of bronze and iron tools crossed the Arctic Circle. Runic (Germanic alphabet) inscriptions on freestanding rocks and stones first appeared during this period. These symbols are believed to be both literate and mystical. The runic alphabet was likely developed in Sweden around 200 B.C., reflecting close ties to both the Roman and Greek alphabets. The runic alphabet's use spread across the region, and it became the alphabet of Scandinavian and Northern Germanic peoples.

Despite contact with outside peoples, the Swedes continued to live in relative isolation. Although numerous kingdoms became important in Europe, including the Kingdom of Uppsala, most Swedes lived in small kingdoms ruled by a chieftain. On occasion, several smaller kingdoms joined together under a more powerful king.

Sweden contains numerous Iron Age sites. Notable are Iron Age stone ships at Forgallaskeppet on Öland and Gannarve Skeppssättning in Gotland. These stone monuments reflect contact by sea with the outside world. Excavations at Eketorps Borg, a fourth-century fort on Öland, have yielded numerous Iron Age artifacts.

THE VIKING AGE

Around A.D. 700, the Vikings began to carve their imprint on Scandinavia and the known world. By A.D. 1000, outside people were using the term Viking to describe seafaring people from the north (Denmark, Norway, and Sweden). Interestingly, in contemporary Ireland, they prefer to use the term "Dane" to describe these people. Appropriately, the Vikings who dominated Western Europe, England, and Ireland were from Norway and Denmark. Sweden's Vikings went to the east and southeast, first dominating the Baltic Region and then extending into Russia, where they dominated the population. Ultimately, their power extended downstream, following the Dnieper River to the Black Sea and the Volga River to the Caspian Sea. From there, Viking influences extended as far south as Sicily, Constantinople, and Baghdad. They were seeking the silver, gold, silk, foodstuffs, slaves, and other treasures of these regions and in turn extended their trade areas.

Geographically, "Viking" is an appropriate term. In Norwegian, the word *vikr* means "fjord" or "inlet," thus the Vikings would be the people of the fjords. In Sweden, *vik* is the word for "bay," thus the Vikings are the people of the bay. By A.D. 800, the Vikings had begun to successfully plunder and rule the outside world. In 793, they attacked England and various small islands, including the Orkneys, and Isle of Man. Ultimately, they gained control of most of England and Ireland.

Vikings from Sweden controlled the rivers of Central Europe and Russia. In Russia, they became known as the *Rus*, which is believed to be the Finnish name for the Vikings. The Vikings controlled the rivers, trade, and peoples of western Russia. Their domination of Europe lasted more than 300 years. Throughout this period, they attacked and occupied foreign lands. Viking ships entered the Mediterranean Sea on the south, and they also sailed west to Iceland and Greenland. Evidence indicates that Vikings under Leif Eriksson reached the east coast of North America in 1001.

Though they were perceived as a people who plundered everything in their path, some of the Vikings' impact on the landscape was positive. For example, they established many forts, ports, and trading communities that ultimately grew into major European cities. Among those urban centers that were initially Viking outposts are Dublin, Ireland; Kiev, Ukraine; and Novgorod, Russia.

The Vikings of Norway and Denmark utilized the North and Norwegian seas as springboards to wealth and power. Sweden's Vikings, known as the Svear, were far from the North Sea, so they traveled instead to the Baltic Region and on to Russia. The Vikings were a well-organized society, with skilled shipbuilders, successful merchants, and a powerful military. Like their western counterparts, the Svears succeeded because they used their resources effectively. Their forests supplied the wood for ships and their foundries the iron ore, then metals, for weapons. Their warships and merchant ships were designed to perform certain tasks, including sailing shallow rivers and treacherous seas and even being able to be transported across land. Central Sweden was an effective starting point for their expeditions because geographically, it was also a well-protected fortress. Often harsh weather, a complex rugged and island-dominated coastline, and its northern location isolated Sweden from outside attack.

Viking expeditions crossed the Baltic Sea as early as the ninth century and established control over areas of present-day Finland, Estonia, Latvia, Lithuania, Russia, Belarus, and Ukraine. Rivers draining into the Baltic Sea provided the Vikings rapid access to the interior of these lands. Once they controlled the waterways, they quickly established control of the local Slav populations, captured their wealth, and then utilized them as slave labor to move their ships overland to other rivers and lakes. By 862, Rurik, a Viking chieftain, had become ruler of the Slavs. He is considered to be the first monarch of Russia and ruled from Novgorod. By 882, Oleg (believed to be Rurik's brother) moved control of the kingdom to Kiev. Igor (believed to be Rurik's son) followed Oleg. Igor is generally credited with establishing the Rurik Dynasty. For more than 700 years, descendants of Rurik and Igor ruled Russia from Kiev and later Moscow. Their dynasty ended in 1598 when Tsar Feodor I died without an heir.

In 988, Vladimir of Kiev sent 6,000 Viking warriors to Byzantium (today's Istanbul, Turkey), in support of his wife's royal family. These warriors, known as the Varangian Guard, protected the emperor and exploited lands to the east for their personal wealth. Interestingly, Vladimir's children became key members of several European monarchies. His son Jaroslav married the Swedish princess Ingegred, whereas his daughters became the queens of France, Hungary, and Norway. Vladimir became a Christian and brought the Slavs into the Russian Orthodox Church. He introduced Byzantine culture to his people and built ornate cathedrals.

Meanwhile, in Sweden, the Vikings thrived. The city of Birka, near Stockholm, functioned for a time as Sweden's most important trade center. It was finally destroyed by the Christian King Olav Haraldsson and his Norwegian/Danish Vikings early in the eleventh century. About the same time, King Olof Skötkonung of Sweden was baptized into Christianity by St. Sigfrid, an English missionary. Slowly, his people abandoned the pagan Viking gods of Thor, Odin, and Frö for the Christian Trinity of Catholicism. The conversion of the Swedish people to Christianity, a process that was started by Ansgar, a German monk, in 829, encompassed more than two centuries.

Agriculture remained the principal means of existence and employment for the Viking Age people who remained in Sweden. Some prospered as merchants and traders, whereas others returned from expeditions with great wealth. Some Viking women went on expeditions as shield girls (skjoldmø), but the Viking married women managed the home. Scandinavian society comprised three social classes—rulers, freemen, and slaves, who could earn their freedom. Nobles and freemen elected governing kings at assemblies called a *ting*. Such councils are still important elements of Scandinavian government.

By 1060, the Viking Age was ending, and Sweden, Norway, and Denmark had become independent kingdoms. In 1101, their borders were defined. The world was changing; the Crusades, Christianity, and nationalism all impacted Viking life. During the Viking Age, Vikings dominated much of the known world. At one time or another, they controlled all or portions of Norway, Sweden, Denmark, and Finland. Their empire extended eastward to include Estonia, Latvia, Lithuania, Russia, and Belarus. Southward and westward, it included Germany, England, Scotland, Ireland, the Hebrides, the Isle of Man, the Orkney Islands, the Shetland Islands, the Faroe Islands, Iceland, Greenland, and Newfoundland. Although not as extensive nor as wealthy as Rome, the Vikings ruled a formidable military empire.

Evidence of Viking civilization still dots Sweden's cultural landscape. At Trelleborg, in southern Gotland a Viking fortress has been rebuilt on its original 1,000-year-old site. Stone ships, grave sites, and meeting sites are located at Ales Stenar, along the Skåne coast, and at Västerås, in Eastern Svealand. An impressive museum at Birka portrays the city in its prime and also includes on-site archaeological digs. Museums and historic sites across the country feature numerous Viking artifacts, including runic stones and materials about their ships. Viking sagas, folktales, gods, and games still play an important part in today's Swedish life.

As Viking domination declined, royalty and Christianity became increasingly important. In the next four centuries, conflicts between powerful nobles and the elected kings brought about a country of weak kings with limited authority.

CHRISTIANITY ARRIVES

Christianity introduced an important cultural feature to the landscape, the stave church. These structures date back to about 1050. Stave churches are of interest to geographers because their materials, design, and construction reflect the physical environment and cultural heritage of the area. These unique structures were built of local woods by people skilled in shipbuilding and wood-carving. Unfortunately, wooden structures generally do not stand the test of time. In Sweden, the only remaining stave church is a sixteenth-century structure located at Hedared. Several stave churches have survived in neighboring Norway. In the United States, a beautiful replica stave church is located in Rapid City, South Dakota.

In the fourteenth century, Sweden was blessed with the presence of St. Birgitta (Bridget), a dynamic married woman who was committed to her faith. St. Brigitta experienced powerful visions about religion and politics. In 1370, she founded the monastic Brigittine Order of nuns. In 1391, she was canonized a saint in the Roman Catholic Church. Devotion to St. Brigitta survived the Reformation, and she has remained the patron saint of Sweden. In 1990, the Roman Catholic Church named St. Brigitta as a "Patron Saint of Europe."

FORGING OF A SWEDISH NATION

By the late 1300s, the royalty of Scandinavia began to intermarry. By doing so, they hoped to strengthen their power bases and resist the influence of the German Hanseatic League merchants, who dominated trade in Scandinavia. King Haakon VI of Norway (son of the King of Sweden) married Queen Margrethe, a Dane. In 1387, Haakon VI died and Queen Margrethe became ruler of Norway. She facilitated the Union of Kalmar in 1397, which united Norway, Sweden, and Denmark under one ruler.

The Vasa Era

In the 1400s, following the death of the Union's King Christopher of Bavaria, a split occurred. Denmark and Norway elected Christian I as their king, causing the loss of Norwegian independence. Sweden elected a nobleman, Karl Knutsson, as King Charles VIII. This resulted in ongoing conflict between Denmark and Sweden. By 1520, Denmark had gained control of much of Sweden. At the Stockholm bloodbath, King Christian II of Denmark had 80 Swedish leaders beheaded. The Swedish people were outraged and sought complete independence. Their cause found a leader in young Gustavus Vasa, who assembled an army that drove the Danes from all except the southern part of Sweden. On June 6, 1523, he became King Gustav I Vasa. That day is celebrated as Sweden's National Day, and he is revered as the founder of modern Sweden.

With Sweden facing financial disaster from war debts, Gustav I Vasa found a source of money through the sale of property he confiscated from the Roman Catholic Church. Denmark and Norway had already converted to Lutheranism, and the faith was also attracting many Swedes. Gustav I Vasa seized the Church's wealth, and established the Swedish Evangelical Lutheran Church as the state religion. Gustav I Vasa imposed strong government control over the people, while utilizing Sweden's agricultural and mineral resources to generate wealth. The country grew and prospered.

Gustav II Adolph served as king of Sweden from 1611 to 1632 and helped his country become an expansionist power in Europe. During his reign, Sweden gained control of much of northern Europe, including Finland, Estonia, Latvia, and parts of Germany and Poland.

The Age of Greatness

In the 1600s under Gustav II Adolph, Sweden became an expansionist power, gaining control over much of Finland and the Baltic states. From 1611 to 1721, Sweden was northern Europe's most powerful nation. This period is known as Sweden's Age of Greatness. During this time, the country prospered economically, politically, and culturally, even though it was at war during much of it. The Peace of Nystad, in 1721, ended the Age of Greatness. By then Sweden had lost more than half of the territory gained by expansionism. Sweden has never again attained the power she held during her Age of Greatness.

The Era of Liberty and Liberalism

Sweden's new constitution of 1719 transferred political control from the monarchy to the *Riksdag* (Parliament). The monarch became a ceremonial position with little influence. The Riksdag comprised four separate assemblies (nobles, priests, burgesses, and peasants), who engaged in a continuous conflict for power. In 1771, King Gustav III led a revolution that briefly restored power to the monarchy. His son Gustav IV Adolph led Sweden into the Napoleonic Wars. In 1809, the army overthrew him, and his uncle Charles XIII became king. That same year, still another constitution was enacted that shared power between the monarch, the parliament, and the government.

Charles XIII died in 1810 without an heir. Sweden's Riksdag, hoping to please Napoleon, invited Prince Jean Baptiste Jules Bernadotte, a French field marshal to become king. He became King Charles XIV John and ruled for 30 years. Thus began Sweden's Bernadotte monarchy, which continues today. Charles XIV John abandoned Napoleon and attacked his ally Denmark. With Napoleon's defeat, Denmark surrendered Norway to Sweden. Charles XIV John then became king of the Union of Sweden and Norway. Although he never learned to speak Swedish or Norwegian, Charles XIV John proved to be a capable ruler and the Union prospered. His descendants led the country through constitutional revisions and social welfare initiatives. Restructuring the Riksdag from four to two elected chambers was an important revision of this time.

HARD TIMES AND EMIGRATION

Beginning in about 1825, the Union of Sweden and Norway experienced substantial emigration of citizens to the

United States. Over the next 100 plus years, hunger, warfare, population pressures, and poverty spirited their migration to America. They fled the rural areas of Sweden and Norway for the fertile American Midwest. Today, their American descendants are found in significant numbers in Midwest states including Minnesota, Ohio, and the Dakotas. Recent Swedish emigrants have settled in the Pacific Northwest and New England areas. Until 1868, U.S. immigration totals counted Sweden and Norway as one country. It is estimated that from 1820 until today, 1.3 million people emigrated from Sweden, and another 900,000 people left Norway for the United States.

THE CONTEMPORARY ERA

In 1905, the Norwegian Storting (parliament) chose to establish Norwegian embassies around the world. Sweden reminded them that Norway was part of the Union. In response, Norway held a national referendum to determine the sentiments of the people. The vote was 368,208 for independence and only 184 for retaining the Union. Sweden reluctantly concurred, and the Kingdom of Norway was re-established. The twentieth century witnessed the emergence of the major political force in Sweden, the Social Democratic Party. It is strongly supported by cooperatives and unions. For more than 100 years, this party has dominated Swedish politics. It has led the development of the Swedish System, the world's most inclusive tax-funded welfare system. During this era, the Riksdag enacted important governmental reforms, including its conversion to a unicameral body (having one legislative chamber) in 1971, universal suffrage, and a new constitution in 1975 that revoked the remaining powers of the monarchy. Sweden upgraded its electrical waterpower facilities and established nuclear power plants to meet energy needs. It also developed laws and programs to enhance industry and establish niches for Swedish products in world trade.

Sweden has been a neutral nation since 1818. During World War I, the country suffered a blockade of its ports that created food shortages and hardship. In World War II, although Norway and Denmark fell to Nazi Germany, Sweden remained neutral. It was forced to allow the German armies to cross its territory, however. At the same time, it sheltered 200,000 war refugees. Following the war, Sweden joined the United Nations, and, in 1953, Swedish diplomat Dag Hammarskjöld was elected Secretary General of the UN. He served in that position for 8 years. Sweden declined membership in the North Atlantic Treaty Organization (NATO) and opposed the War in Vietnam and the Gulf Wars. However, in 1994, it did vote to join the European Union (EU), despite concerns that membership might compromise its neutrality. Sweden entered the EU on January 1, 1995, and to date its neutrality remains intact.

SUMMARY

The cultural history of Sweden has displayed interesting changes relative to its role as a people and nation. Twice in its history, Sweden achieved recognition as a military power, first through Viking conquests and second during its Age of Greatness. During these periods, Sweden dominated vast regions beyond its traditional borders, and exploited weaker peoples. Today, however, Sweden is a neutral nation, deeply committed to its unique capitalistic social welfare society. Sweden has established an excellent standard of living for its people. As a nation, it is also committed to facilitating world peace.

The cultural landscape of contemporary Sweden incorporates historical traditions and artifacts of past generations in a progressive contemporary industrial welfare nation. The resulting cultural landscape reflects the uniqueness of Sweden.

4

People and Culture

The third course of the smorgasbord features cold dishes, but differs from the two previous courses because it essentially celebrates foods of the land. Popular cold dishes in this course include boiled ham, smoked ham, roast beef, veal, pâtés, smoked eel, tomato and lettuce salads, apple sauce, pickles, beetroot, radishes, and mustard. Breads, crispbreads, and Swedish cheeses are available throughout the smorgasbord.

Just as the third course celebrates the foods of the land, this chapter celebrates the people and culture of the land. It examines characteristics of the population, their health and safety, and their migration patterns and diversity. It also notes the festivals and feasts that inspire celebrations such as the smorgasbord.

POPULATION

Sweden's population density is closely related to the landscape and the sea. The country has an average density of about 50 people per square mile (20 people per square kilometer) of land. This is not a heavily populated landscape. It is only about two-thirds that of the United States. Highest densities occur in the warmer and more fertile southern part of the country. Lowest densities, as you might expect, stretch across the colder and more rugged areas of northern Norrland.

Historically the people of Sweden have lived in both rural and urban areas. Today, the population is heavily urbanized. Interestingly, Sweden's 21 counties are relatively equal in population distribution. Only one county, Gotland, has a population of less than 100,000. The most populated counties are Stockholm, with more than 1.8 million residents, Västra Gotalands with almost 1.5 million people, and Skåne with more than 1.15 million residents. The counties with the lowest populations tend to be in the extreme north and the extreme southeast. Urbanization, relatively new to Sweden, has grown consistently since the 1930s. With the extensive development of urban apartment buildings, nearly 85 percent of all Swedes now live in urban areas.

Sweden's population is no longer being replaced by births and deaths. Instead, the current population growth is a result of increased immigration. This is true throughout much of Europe, as the fertility rate for most European countries is now below the replacement level (2.1 births per woman). Fewer births result in a rapidly aging European population. The fertility rate in Sweden is 1.53 percent, which is one of the lowest in Europe. The failure of Sweden's population to replace itself is also reflected by the death rate that exceeds the birth rate by 0.7 persons per 1,000 population. Therefore, immigration accounts for Sweden's actual population growth.

HEALTH CARE AND SOCIAL SERVICES

Sweden's unique commitment to health care and social services can be traced to the government of Per Albin

Hansson. In the 1930s, he sought to provide economic and social security for all Swedes through a tax system based upon ability to pay. This effort grew into the Swedish System, the world's most inclusive tax-funded welfare system. It is sometimes referred to as "the third way," an option that differs from capitalism or communism. The Swedish System considers all people as equals and all citizens equally entitled to security and well-being.

From cradle to grave, the government provides all families with services, security, and care. This system consists of virtually free health care that begins with maternity and birth and ends with death. Included are government-subsidized medicines, hospital care, dental care, sick pay, and elder care.

The educational system includes free or government-assisted day care and preschools, free elementary and secondary schooling, and significant government funding for the university and adult education levels. The system also includes government-financed housing, a monthly child allowance, unemployment benefits, parental insurance, social aid, and pensions.

In recent years the tremendous costs of these programs have put great pressure on the government and taxpayers. There are concerns and complaints about a lack of personnel in many program offices, waiting lists for certain medical procedures, and inadequate capitalization of pension funds. Even with these problems, the Swedish public continues to demand the services and endeavors to protect the system.

Today, Sweden strongly supports equal rights for all people. The rights of women and children and of individuals with physical handicaps or mental disorders are protected. In addition, discrimination based on sexual preference, ethnic origin, religious beliefs, or political conviction is prohibited.

The polis (police force) is responsible for safety. Sweden is a relatively safe country with low crime rates. In many small towns and rural areas, the police stations are closed in the evenings. The greatest likelihood of a crime occurring is in larger cities. Private security officers are employed in retail centers, at railroad stations, and at industrial sites. At night, it is generally safe to walk the streets of the larger cities. Exceptions are urban areas where drugs and alcohol may be present.

EMIGRATION AND IMMIGRATION

From 1820 to 1940, 34.5 million Europeans immigrated to the United States. Ireland, Norway, and Sweden provided the greatest proportions of any one country's population to this number. More than 1.3 million Swedes moved to the United States during that time.

Emigration from Sweden to the United States dates back to the 1630s, when the government sent colonists to establish New Sweden in modern-day Delaware. This settlement failed, but was a precursor of things to come. The greatest exodus of people from Sweden occurred between 1840 and 1920, and their migration was primarily to the United States. Most emigrants came from poor, overpopulated farmlands in the south. Some left to avoid the military draft, whereas many were sharecroppers or hired farm workers looking for opportunity in America.

From 1860 to 1880, Sweden experienced crop failures, depression, and a declining standard of living. Free and open lands, jobs, railroad propaganda, and letters from friends in the United States made emigration very appealing to the landless farmer. The Homestead Act of 1862 was the ultimate attraction. This Federal legislation offered homesteaders an opportunity to own 160 acres of farmland. In America, the Swedish emigrants primarily settled in the Middle West from Ohio to the Dakotas, with the greatest concentration in Minnesota. Swedish immigration to the United States virtually shut down in the 1920s with changes in the U.S. immigration policy. Interestingly, Sweden also benefited from emigrants who returned home from America bringing their wealth, experiences, and new ideas.

Today, over 11.5 percent of Sweden's population comprises foreign-born immigrants. Immigration to Sweden began in earnest following World War II. The first such immigrants were war orphans from Finland. For the next 25 years, immigrants from Finland and Yugoslavia came to Sweden seeking jobs, wealth, or safety. Today, the greatest numbers of new residents are coming from Eastern Europe. The Finns and Yugoslavs continue to immigrate in significant numbers, as do Poles, Turks, and Hungarians. Outside of Europe, the largest number of immigrants come from the Middle East (Iraq and Iran), and Asia (India, Vietnam, and Thailand). Peoples from Chile, Somalia, and Ethiopia also add to the immigration numbers and the diversity of Sweden's population. The country also continues to welcome some Americans as immigrants.

To become a Swedish citizen, immigrants must live in the country for five years before applying for citizenship. However, immigrants from Norway, Finland, Denmark, and Iceland require only two years of residence for citizenship. Not all who come to Sweden to work plan on becoming citizens. Some come as guest workers intending to stay only until they amass some wealth, so they can return to their homeland. Both immigrants and guest workers enjoy immediate access to most of Sweden's social and welfare programs.

SAMI

Among the nine million residents of Sweden are 15,000 indigenous people known as the Sami (Saami; Lapps). For thousands of years, the Sami have lived in the northern part of present-day Norway, Sweden, Finland and extreme northwestern Russia. Today, an estimated 55,000 to 75,000 Sami people live in Sápmi (Lappland), which comprises parts of the Scandinavian Peninsula, Finland, and Russia. More than half of all Sami now live in Norway. Although it is difficult to determine actual populations for a traditionally mobile culture

The Sami people live throughout northern Sweden. About 10 to 15 percent of Sweden's Sami are reindeer herders.

occupying parts of four countries, most estimate that about 25 percent of the Sami live in Sweden.

Most people think of the Sami as being reindeer herders. In reality, they are a far more complicated society. In fact, only 10 percent to 15 percent of Sweden's Sami are involved in reindeer herding. Traditionally, these indigenous people were closely tied to nature and functioned as hunters, fishers, herders, and boatbuilders. Today, many still earn their living in that manner, but others combine and mix traditional work activities with native handicrafts, small-scale farming, mining, and tourism. Still others left Sápmi, and moved into Stockholm and other larger centers, where they gained employment in business, industry, and the services.

Since the seventeenth century, Sweden has initiated actions and policies that have resulted in economic, social, and political intrusions into Sami lands. In many ways, these intrusions parallel similar policies and actions toward native cultures throughout the world. The governments of Norway, Finland, and Sweden, have all taken control of Sápmi lands within their borders, administered them, and opened them for development. Sweden believes that their free and open society has not oppressed the Sami, but many Sami believe that despite the benefits of Swedish society, their culture and society have long been oppressed by the government.

In the 1600s, Sweden first infringed upon Sápmi's enormous deposits of natural resources. The land was opened to exploration, settlement, and ownership by non-Sami people. During the last 400 years, new roads have been built, communities established, and Swedish people have assumed ownership of the lands. Additionally, Swedish government, economics, education, culture, and society were introduced to (or imposed upon) the Sami.

Generally, when indigenous people become dominated by other governments or cultures, numerous changes occur in the lives of the people. The Sami have been no exception. For thousands of years, they were a hunting people who depended largely on wild reindeer as their primary source of food and clothing. In the last 400 years, the Sami have changed to herding domesticated reindeer. As the reindeer herds, both wild and domesticated, migrated across the Sápmi, so did the Sami. Unfortunately, for the Sami, the Swedish government did not recognize their ownership rights to the Sápmi. Instead, Sweden has claimed ownership of Sápmi land, water, forests, minerals, and even hunting. These conditions have severely changed the Sami's traditionally nomadic way of life.

Until recently, Sami children were not provided the same educational opportunities as were other Swedish youngsters. The government limited the Sami to more elementary or basic educational programs. Governmental policies and actions essentially split the Sami into two peoples. There were those who were granted rights involved with reindeer herding and those the government attempted to assimilate into Swedish society.

Since 1993, the Sami people have assumed a more active role in determining their destiny. In that year, the Sami Parliament was established, with 31 popularly elected Members of Parliament. The Sami Parliament functions in two areas, one with some state authorities and the second as a political body. The Sami Parliament, with Swedish governmental approval, has the following responsibilities:

1. Distributing state subsidies to Sami people

2. Providing compensation for predator losses to reindeer herders

3. Developing the social progress of the Sami

4. Forwarding an agenda to improve Sami land and water rights

5. Enhancing social, educational, and economic opportunities

6. Maintaining Sami culture

Despite the activities of the Sami Parliament, disagreements between the Sami people and the Swedish government continue to occur and will likely continue into the future.

Today, across Sápmi, the Sami are experiencing a cultural revitalization. The *kofte,* or traditional Sami clothes, are worn not only in the Sami homeland, but also in other areas of Scandinavia. Throughout Sápmi and Scandinavia, one will find Sami movies, Sami language books and magazines, and recordings and performances of native music. Particularly important to this revitalization is the music of Mari Boine Persen, a Sami vocalist, whose popular music is helping to spread the Sami language throughout the region.

FEASTS AND FESTIVALS

Swedish people love festivals and holidays. It has been said that "when the Swedes left Catholicism for Lutheranism, they abandoned everything except the holidays." Like all humor, there is some truth to that statement. The Swedes have established a unique blending of cultural, religious, and secular practices in their national celebrations.

Christmas is Sweden's most important feast and holiday. The celebration begins with Advent, intensifies with St. Lucia's Day, Christmas Eve, and Christmas Day, and ends with the feast of the Epiphany. St. Lucia Day is celebrated on December 13. Young girls awaken early, dress in white gowns, and don a crown of leaves and lighted candles. Dressed as St. Lucia, they awaken the rest of the family with song about darkness and the coming daylight. Each family's St. Lucia then serves coffee and Lucia buns. On that day throughout Sweden, the celebration is repeated with thousands of St. Lucias bringing light to others through plays, songs, and food at schools, work, and at community parades.

Food and drink are important throughout the Christmas celebrations, especially drinking glögg, a potent wine, and eating gingerbread cookies. In Sweden, children open their presents from Father Christmas on Christmas Eve. On Christmas Day, Swedish families celebrate the feast with a *Julbord* (Yule smorgasbord) dinner. New Year's Eve celebrations are similar to those in America. The Feast of the Epiphany marks the end of the Christmas period.

Easter is another major religious feast. The Resurrection of Jesus Christ is celebrated throughout the land. A uniquely Swedish aspect of the feast is Easter Eve, when children dress as witches and go from house to house trading their drawings for treats.

Easter is followed by Walpurgis Day, on April 30. This day celebrates both the feast of St. Walburga and a pagan Viking spring feast. College students celebrate Walpurgis Day with a festival to welcome the coming of spring. The festival includes music, floats, parades, speeches, dancing, choirs, and bonfires. April 30 is also the King's birthday. Traditionally, children travel to Stockholm to present the king with freshly picked wildflowers.

Midsummer's Eve is another festival with Viking roots. It is held at the end of June when the country's vegetation is lush and sunshine lasts almost all day long. Everything, including buildings and vehicles, is decorated with flowers. In communities throughout the country, garland-covered maypoles are raised in the afternoon and family and friends circle around them dancing and singing traditional songs. A feast of herring, new potatoes, strawberries, schnapps, and beer complete the Midsummer's Eve Festival.

The Swedes enjoy these major festivals, as well as many smaller celebrations. Among these are traditional crayfish parties with family and friends celebrated in late August. In other parts of Sweden, surstromming (sour herring) or eel parties are held. In the fall, people celebrate the outdoors by walking and hiking through the multicolored countryside. They also enjoy moose and deer hunting, as well as picking wild berries and mushrooms. St. Martin's Day, on November 10, is traditionally celebrated with a dinner of cooked goose and black soup (goose blood soup).

SUMMARY

The lush forests and northern climes help explain Sweden's population distribution. The people of Sweden have achieved a unique place among the world's nations. Sweden has lost more than 1.3 million people to emigration over the last 175 years. It has survived these emigration losses only to face new obligations resulting from today's large immigrant population. Sweden has established effective programs and services that address the health and safety of its citizens. Sweden, like neighboring Norway, is committed to enhancing Sami culture.

The Midsummer's Eve Festival is held annually at the end of June and is one of the most popular celebrations in Sweden. Throughout the country, people dance and sing traditional songs, as they circle around garland-covered maypoles.

Throughout history, the people of Sweden have valued their progress and culture. This pride continues to be demonstrated today through the joyous celebrations that occur during Sweden's festivals and feast. Today, the people of Sweden celebrate with pride both their country's history of progress as well as their country's commitment to equality for all people.

5

Government of Sweden

Our next course in the smorgasbord features hot dishes. Hot dishes, a recent addition to the smorgasbord, became increasingly popular in the twentieth century, following the emergence of restaurants and the Aga stove. The Aga stove, a continuous cooker, was invented in 1922 by Sweden's Dr. Gustav Dalén, a Nobel Prize-winning physicist. This stove, now found in more than 750,000 homes worldwide, enables the hostess to keep food hot until needed. Among the more popular hot dishes in a smorgasbord are Swedish meatballs, Jansson's Temptation (anchovies & potatoes), reindeer fillet, sausages, minced beef, kidneys, a variety of omelets, and baked vegetables. Just as the introduction of the Aga stove enhanced the smorgasbord, the governmental programs of Sweden have enhanced the well-being of all its citizens.

The Swedish government's commitment to its citizens to be "the home of the people," helps us to understand much of its political geography. Because of this ongoing commitment, Sweden has become the world's foremost welfare society. Residents are provided a wide array of social welfare benefits and programs, each designed to meet a specific need from cradle to grave. This system also plays a vital role in Sweden's international efforts, including those involving the European Union, the United Nations, and especially world trade.

SOCIAL WELFARE

The Scandinavian countries have all made major commitments to the social welfare of their citizenry. In Sweden, Norway, Denmark, and Finland, the welfare commitment is entwined throughout all aspects of government and daily life. Although most European nations have established social welfare programs, most focus on one or two services, such as social security, health care, or education. These programs pale in comparison to the social welfare programs of the Scandinavian countries.

Sweden, under the leadership of the long-ruling Social Democratic Party, has developed one of the world's most comprehensive social welfare systems. It is often referred to as "the Swedish System," or "the home of the people." Sweden imposes an extensive tax burden on businesses and individuals to fund their otherwise virtually free welfare system. The Swedish System provides the people free and universal access to education, child care, health care, elder care, unemployment insurance, pensions, and a variety of other social and economic services. Every Swedish citizen has equal access to social welfare programs. Rich or poor, employed or unemployed, citizen or immigrant, everyone enjoys equal access. This is available in all areas of the country, from urban Stockholm to remote Mittådalen.

In recent years, economic hardships have negatively impacted Sweden's welfare model. The economic downturn of the early 1990s placed serious financial burdens on the system. Part of the burden resulted from high unemployment, particularly among the immigrant residents. Immigrants usually encompass only 11 percent of the population, but during the downturn, they accounted for nearly half of the social assistance expenditures. The Swedish people are engaged in debate about this issue. Some would like to reduce benefits for immigrants; however, the population as a whole strongly supports maintaining the existing system.

Taxation is the means by which Sweden finances its extensive social welfare program. The benefits and services provided include medical care, maternity, elder care, and burial expenses. The Swedish worker's salary is taxed significantly to support these programs. Although costly, the average Swedish citizen believes in this social welfare system. They trust that the "home of the people" will continue into the future. They are convinced that their grandchildren and great-grandchildren will be willing to meet the tax needs in order to assure continued benefits for all.

SWEDISH SYSTEM OF GOVERNMENT

Sweden's governmental system evolved over time, but throughout its history the people have valued some form of assembly as being vital to good government. Such assemblies (Tings) existed during the Viking Age and have continued into the present. Even during the reign of Sweden's strongest monarchies, the assemblies were convened. At one point four separate and very independent national assemblies governed Sweden. Today, Sweden is governed by one national assembly, with numerous regional and local assemblies involved at lower levels of government.

The 1719 Constitution created the Riksdag, the Swedish parliament, and a democratic monarchy based upon the "British Model." In 1809, a new constitution divided control of Sweden among the king, the government, and the parliament. Over time, the monarchy's executive role lessened to ceremonial status, and the Riksdag achieved complete control over all legislation. The Riksdag has the responsibility of electing the prime minister, amending the constitution, passing laws, and allocating state funds.

In 1975, a constitutional change converted the Riksdag to a unicameral parliament. As a result, the Swedes elect the 349 members of the Riksdag every four years. Members come from 29 different regions or constituencies across the country. The number of elected seats varies with the population of each constituency, with an average being 10 to 12 members. With variations in population size, however, the number will range from highly urbanized Stockholm County, with 39 members, to rural Gotland County, with only 2 members.

The elected prime minister forms a cabinet and operates the executive responsibilities assigned by the Riksdag. The cabinet, or executive branch, comprises the prime minister, department ministers, and ministers without portfolios. This cabinet oversees more than 300 agencies and public administrations. The executive branch of the government proposes new laws to the Riksdag and also implements the legislation. The survival of the executive branch depends upon the confidence of the Riksdag. A vote of no confidence will force elections and administrative change.

Seven political parties are represented in the Riksdag: Social Democrats, Moderates, Liberals, Christian Democrats, Leftists, Centre, and the Green. The Social Democratic Party, built with labor union support, has traditionally been the most powerful political force in Sweden. The Moderates are interested in smaller government, whereas the Liberals support more government, with more social welfare programs. Protestant-based Christian Democrats follow a more conservative line, and the Left Party is the contemporary name for the Communist Party. Centre Party support is predominantly rural, whereas the Green Party draws its support from environmentalists. Numerous smaller parties also participate in elections but with little national success.

The House of Parliament in Stockholm is home to the Riksdag, Sweden's governing body. Seven political parties are represented in the Riksdag: Social Democrats, Moderates, Liberals, Christian Democrats, Leftists, Centre, and the Green.

The king serves as the formal head of state. In this capacity, he has ceremonial duties that include chairing the Advisory Council on Foreign Affairs, meeting with foreign dignitaries, representing Sweden internationally, and opening the annual session of the Riksdag. He has no political powers and remains free of any politics. The monarchy is inherited. The oldest child of the incumbent monarch is first in line to succeed. King Carl XVI Gustaf has reigned as Sweden's Head of State since 1973.

Sweden has a constitutionally guaranteed independent judicial system. Judges are appointed by the government, and their appointments are generally permanent. There are two types of court, general courts and special courts. General courts include district courts, appellate courts, and the Supreme Court, as well as general administrative courts, which duplicate all three courts at the county level. Almost all litigation begins with the general district court. This court's decisions may be challenged in one of the six courts of appeal. As a last resort, court decisions can be appealed to the 16 Justices of the Supreme Court.

The administrative courts focus on cases between the individual and public authorities. Such disputes are often based on tax disputes, minor children, drug or alcohol problems, mental illness, social welfare, and insurance matters. Most of these cases are at the local county level. Several specialized courts operate judicially. These include the Labor Court, Market Court, and Rent Tribunal. Some of these specialized courts are integrated with the general courts, and others are entirely independent.

Sweden is also governed at the regional and local levels. Regional government is organized within 21 counties. The government functions through elected county councils and county administrative boards. On the local level, 290 municipalities (kommuner) function with elected decision-making municipal councils. Each municipal council appoints a local executive board that administers all local programs and agencies. In recent years, the central government has transferred more and more authority to the local and regional governments, with the belief that the closer to the people, the better the government.

SWEDEN'S EXTERNAL RELATIONS

In the 1950s, the foundation for the European Union (EU) began with the establishment of the European Steel and Coal Community. Six countries—Belgium, the Netherlands, Luxembourg, France, Germany, and Italy—agreed to allow the movement of coal and steel across their borders without taxes, tariffs, or quotas. This agreement assured the participants inexpensive access to each other's coal and steel resources. Today, this cooperative agreement has evolved into the European Union, a group of European countries that have mutually opened their borders to each other, established joint governmental and economic programs, and allowed the free movement of goods and people.

When formed in 1992, the European Union (EU) focused primarily on trade. Since then, the EU has developed leadership and policies in many other areas. These include agriculture, industry, regionalism, tourism, planning, economic development, and health and safety issues. The European Union is also involved with governmental concerns that include immigration, foreign policy, the death penalty, and the establishment of a military force.

In 1973, Denmark, the United Kingdom, and Ireland joined the original six members of the European Union. Then in 1981, Greece joined the EU, followed in 1986 by Spain and Portugal. By 1995, with the addition of Austria, Finland, and Sweden, the European Union had expanded to 15 members.

The EU has established a monetary system based on the *euro*. Twelve of the 15 original members utilize the euro as their monetary system. Only the United Kingdom, Denmark, and Sweden have not adopted it. European Union monetary matters are conducted through the European Central Bank in Frankfurt, Germany.

Recently, ten other European countries have joined the EU. The new members are Cyprus, the Czech Republic, Estonia, Hungary, Latvia, Lithuania, Malta, Poland, the Slovak Republic, and Slovenia. Five other countries are at various stages of consideration for future membership: Bulgaria, Romania, Turkey, Croatia, and the former Yugoslav Republic of Macedonia. Becoming an EU member requires a lengthy process and intensive investigations. It also requires that laws

Sweden became part of the 25-member European Union in 1995, but has yet to adopt the EU's currency, the *euro*. Pictured here are signs in Stockholm that state "Vote YES" in support of adopting the *euro* at the time of the government's referendum in September 2003. Despite support from most of the country's political parties, Swedish voters shot down the referendum by a wide margin.

be changed to conform to those of the EU. Finally, the citizens of the country must vote in support of membership.

The European Union holds the promise of great opportunities for its member countries. As it develops, however, the EU faces numerous ongoing challenges from its traditionally independent member states. There will be periods of progress and problems, but over time, the EU hopes to achieve its unifying goals.

In 1953, the United States established diplomatic relations with the European Steel and Coal Community. Today, although the United States continues to maintain long-established political, economic, social, and military relations with individual European nations, it also turns to the EU as a major partner in world leadership.

The Nobel Prizes awarded yearly are renowned worldwide. Alfred Nobel, a Swedish scientist, made provisions in his will to establish and fund these esteemed awards. When he died in 1895, Sweden and Norway were united. Swedish by birth, Nobel assigned the responsibility of selecting the prizewinners in science and literature to organizations in his homeland. At the same time, he specifically designated that the Norwegian Storting (parliament), would be responsible for choosing the Nobel Peace Prize winners. Each year, the Storting appoints the committee that selects the winners of the Nobel Peace Prize, with the winner announced on December 10. Yearly, since his death in 1895, international prizes in science and literature, as well as the Nobel Peace Prize have been awarded.

SUMMARY

Sweden has a distinguished history of participatory government. From the age of the Vikings to the present, Sweden's assemblies have provided the people a voice in government. This has shaped an efficient governmental system with a commitment to equality and the well-being of its citizens. Sweden plays an integral role in the capitalist global economy. It is actively committed to the United Nations and to the emerging European Union. Sweden supports its commitment to neutrality and world peace through its joint involvement with Norway in the awarding of the annual Nobel Peace Prize.

CHAPTER

6

Sweden's Economy

We complete our smorgasbord meal with a final course of desserts. Although the sweets are tempting, it is often challenging to find room for more food. Traditionally, the dessert selections include fruit salads, fruits in syrups, and light pastries. Other desserts include pancakes, apple cake, cheesecake with cloudberries, and rosehip soup. After enjoying beer or water throughout the meal, some people prefer coffee or aquavit with dessert.

The dessert dishes challenge us with their rich flavors as we attempt to find room for this course. The economy is also challenging, because its components are part of a complex process that promises rich rewards. This chapter explains how Sweden has become a major player in the world economy. Sweden's wealth results from the effective use of its resources, the development of world-class industries, and extensive welfare and service systems.

Sweden, like all nations, is part of the world's global capitalist economy. The nations of the world vary greatly in their economic structure. At one extreme are those countries in which the government owns and controls all aspects of the economy; at the other end of the continuum are those systems in which the government plays a very minor economic role. Somewhere between the two extremes of this continuum lie countries such as Sweden and the United States.

A geographer gains insight into the government's involvement in the economy by noting the proportion that taxes play in that country's gross domestic production (total value of goods and services per year). For example, tax receipts account for 29.6 percent of the American gross domestic product (GDP). In Sweden, however, tax receipts account for 54.2 percent of the country's GDP. These figures help us to understand that in Sweden the government is far more directly involved in the economy than is the United States government. We will view both the traditional and the modern economy to better understand the role of the government in the Swedish economy.

TRADITIONAL ECONOMIC ACTIVITIES

Sweden's traditional economy originated with the first human beings to reach the Scandinavian Peninsula. These ancient ancestors of the Sami were a hunting and fishing people who followed the migratory reindeer herds to Sápmi after the Ice Age.

Reindeer Herding

Today, many Sami continue to base their economy on the reindeer, with herding replacing most of the hunting. This economy, like the Sami way of life, is facing numerous challenges while struggling to survive in the modern world.

It is estimated that Sweden is home to 230,000 reindeer. These herds migrate to higher elevations for summer grazing and then, with their newly born offspring, return to the lower elevations for the winter. An estimated 26,000 reindeer live in "wild" herds, whereas the remaining 204,000 are domesticated. In Sweden, about 80,000 reindeer a year are processed for meat. Reindeer meat, lean with a gamy taste, is consumed throughout Scandinavia.

Although reindeer herding is an exclusive right of the Sami, the industry faces many challenges. These include restrictions on crossing private lands and the infrastructures of civilization, restrictive governmental controls, profitability, and legal challenges to grazing rights. Despite all these challenges, reindeer herding remains an essential part of Sami life and many view it as the keystone to their cultural survival.

Russia's 1986 Chernobyl nuclear accident had an impact on the Sami and much of Sweden. About one-third of the Sami reindeer herd was slaughtered because of nuclear contamination. Sweden cleared and burned over 700 square miles of contaminated land. Most likely, more negative impacts of the Chernobyl disaster will emerge for years to come in Sweden and elsewhere throughout northwestern Europe.

Fishing

Fishing has been vital to Sweden's economy and food supply for thousands of years. Sweden's geographic location is favorable to the fishing industry. It is adjacent to the Gulf of Bothnia, the Baltic Sea, and the North Sea, and close to the rich fisheries of the northeastern Atlantic Ocean. Inland, Sweden is drained by numerous streams and dotted by thousand of freshwater lakes.

Sweden's fishing fleet yields a diverse catch of seafood. By species, the most important fish caught are cod, herring, sprat, salmon, whiting, shrimp, and Norway lobster. Economically, herring and cod dominate the production of fish for human consumption. Almost equally important economically is the wide variety of fish caught for reduction, rather than food. These species are reduced to fish meal for livestock feed, fish oil, and other by-products.

Commercial fishing requires a tremendous financial investment. The Swedish fleet is small and declining in size. The costly vessels are independently owned and subject to strict governmental regulations by both Sweden and the European Union. In the last 12 years, half the fleet has left the industry.

Aquaculture, or fish farming, has been a growing industry in Sweden despite a recent downturn in sites and production. Rainbow trout, blue mussels, and Arctic char are the most important species in aquaculture production.

Inland resources provide a potential growth area for Sweden's fishing industry. The country is blessed with lakes and streams favorable to fish and fishermen. About three million people fish the lakes and streams each year. The fisherman's family consumes most of the catch. The major species of the inland catch are trout, grayling, salmon, pike, char, and some eel.

Fishing in Sweden is viewed as both an important production industry and a renewable resource. The National Board of Fishing regulates this industry. The two most important segments of the fishing industry are production for human consumption (70 percent) and production for animal feed (30 percent).

Agriculture

Sweden's highly developed agriculture makes excellent use of arable (farmable) land. The amount of arable land in Sweden has increased with the draining of wetlands, and the subsequent plowing of drained lands and grassy meadow areas. Further expansion of forests and farmlands is being challenged by the government, as it seeks to protect and restore meadowlands.

The more than 80,000 Swedish farmers represent about 2 percent of the total population. An additional 60,000

Today, 7 percent of the land—approximately 6.9 million acres—in Sweden is suitable for agricultural use. Crops such as barley, wheat, oats, and hay (pictured here) are harvested by the country's more than 80,000 farmers.

people are employed in the food processing and manufacturing industries. Today, 7 percent of the land in Sweden, or about 6,900,000 acres (2.8 million hectares), is suitable for agricultural use.

Sweden's principal grain crops are barley, wheat, and oats. Grain production occurs throughout the land, but the greatest yields are in the southern areas. Grasses and legumes are grown for livestock forage and feed. Recently, Sweden has experienced an increase in sugar beet production and a declining potato crop. In the south, Sweden's horticulture industry utilizes extensive greenhouses. These farmers produce vegetables, fruits, flowers, and garden plants for local consumption and export.

Livestock also play a vital role in Sweden's agricultural industry. The principal animals are cattle (beef and dairy cows), pigs, chickens, sheep, and horses. Sweden has about 1.7 million head of cattle, about 40 percent of which are dairy cows. The almost 2.3 million pigs reflect the importance of pork in Sweden's food consumption. A vibrant poultry industry operates, with more than 8.5 million chickens being raised for egg and meat production at any time. Sheep and horses are of far less importance.

Swedish farmers are faced with increasing investment costs and strict governmental regulation. Many farmers find it necessary to work other jobs to support their family. They have found employment in forestry, transportation, tourism, and industry.

Many Swedish farmers are active participants in cooperative societies and organizations. These cooperatives are most prevalent in the dairy industry, livestock slaughter, and grain markets. Virtually all of Sweden's dairy industry operates through farmer co-op-owned dairies. Swedish Meats, a cooperative venture, manages almost two-thirds of the livestock slaughter. Finally, a significant portion of the country's grains are marketed through co-ops.

Sweden is a self-sufficient agricultural nation, producing the foods needed to sustain its population. Swedish farmers produce more than $5 billion worth of food products each year. The excess production of fish, dairy products, meats, candies, tobacco, vodka, and grain products are exported to other nations. Interestingly, Sweden's food imports exceed the exports in value, because the Swedish enjoy eating many foods produced in other climates. These include imported fruits and vegetables, coffee and cocoa, fish, processed meats and cheese, beverages, rice, soybeans, and tobacco. Sweden imports more coffee and bananas per capita than any other country.

Forestry

Sweden's forests comprise dominant coniferous trees (85 percent), primarily spruce and pine, and lesser deciduous trees (15 percent) of birch, aspen, and other species. More than 90 percent of the woodland harvest is from coniferous trees. Spruce and pine are cut for saw woods, pulp and paper fiber, and wood processing. The forest industry employs 12 percent of the labor force and produces 20 percent of Sweden's income from exports.

Forests in Sweden thrive under a series of strict governmental regulations. In 1905, the government began regulating both the forest cut and wood consumption. It also established programs to reestablish and revitalize the forests. The result is a thriving sustainable industry that in one year grows 30 percent more wood than it harvests. As a result, the forested area of Sweden has increased during the past century. Farmers and individuals own more than half of the forests. The remaining half is divided between commercial forest companies and Sveaskog AB, a government-owned forest product corporation that is also Sweden's largest land owner.

The forest economy includes three industrial segments: saw wood, pulp and paper, and wood products. In the 1800s, Sweden began cutting the forests of Norrland to feed the sawmills of wood processing companies. Trees were cut and floated downriver to mills. Prosperous sawmills bought vast amounts of forest land from farmers, and then cut the trees for export to other European countries.

Saw wood industries produce a variety of products, including roundwood (logs and poles), wood fuel, and lumber for construction. Recently, saw lumber has increased in economic value through the sales of veneers and engineered woods. The second segment of Sweden's forest economy is the pulp and paper industry. Its products range from pulp for newsprint to high-grade papers, cartonboard, and manufactured fibers. The final segment of Sweden's forest industry is wood products. More than 7,000 companies produce wooden products that include joinery products (flooring, windows, and cabinetry), prefabricated housing, and furniture manufacturing. The manufacturing of Swedish design furniture continues to grow in importance because of worldwide demand. This segment of the industry adds the most significant value to Sweden's forest industry. The forest industry requires a large transportation infrastructure, supporting services, and access to world markets.

Mining

Sweden's mining economy includes metallic minerals, industrial minerals, and mineral fuels. Metallic minerals define Sweden's modern industrial economy. Industrial minerals and fuels are primarily of local importance.

Although neighboring Norway is noted for petroleum, Sweden is the most important metallic mineral producer in Europe. Its metallic minerals include iron ore, gold, lead, zinc, silver, copper, nickel, and molybdenum. Historically, mining in Sweden has focused on iron ore and copper. Today, Swedish mining accounts for 95 percent of the iron ore, 66 percent of the silver, and 46 percent of the lead produced in Europe. It also produces substantial amounts of Europe's copper, gold, and zinc production. Mineral production is centered in Norrland. High-grade iron ore is mined at Kiruna, Malmberget, and Boliden. Other mining areas include: Aitik and Falun (copper), Vehkavaara (gold and copper), and Bergslagen (gold, silver, and zinc). Sweden also has extensive uranium reserves.

Sweden's industrial minerals are used as building stone, construction materials, and sand and gravel. Notable uses include granite for buildings and monuments, limestone for cement and fertilizers, and sandstone for construction. Feldspar is utilized in Sweden's famous glassware and ceramics industries.

Sweden, unlike Norway, is not rich in petroleum and natural gas. Sweden's only mineral fuel is peat, which is partially decayed vegetation that can be dried and burned. Peat is cut for fuel and for agricultural purposes. Sweden must import petroleum, natural gas, and coal for industries. However, Sweden does use local resources to generate energy. Wood is utilized for heat, particularly in homes, and Sweden uses uranium and hydropower to generate electricity.

Sweden is also committed to producing energy from biomass. The term *biomass* refers to any plant-derived organic matter available on a renewable basis. Biomass technologies may help move Sweden's economy to a more sustainable energy source with less reliance on fossil fuels.

THE MODERN ECONOMY

Sweden's traditional economy began with hunting, fishing, and collecting food. During the industrial revolution, the economy grew to include forestry and mining. The foundation of Sweden's modern economy is threefold: the forestry industry; iron and steel; and electric power industries. All other aspects of Sweden's contemporary economy rest on this foundation.

Forest Industry

The forest industry, part of the traditional economy explained earlier in this chapter, is also an important segment of Sweden's modern economy. As the twentieth century approached, Sweden's economy was dominated by the wealth and power of the forest barons, who exploited the north. The barons' wealth, combined with the country's natural resources, helped to facilitate the development of many new industries. The forest products industry today accounts for 15 percent of Sweden's exports, primarily as pulp, paper, and furniture.

Iron and Steel Industries

Iron and steel formed another cornerstone of Sweden's industrial base. This industry began in central Sweden with blast furnaces and hammer forges. By the eighteenth century, iron ore was extracted and smelted with charcoal to produce high-quality commercial iron and steel. At that time, Sweden was producing one-third of the world's iron.

Sweden manufactures "Swedish Steel," which is widely recognized as the world's highest in quality. The lack of coal in Sweden is largely responsible for this distinction. Without coal, Sweden relied upon electric power for smelting. This produced a higher quality steel than that produced by coal smelting in other countries. Over time, new technologies, external competition, the aforementioned lack of coal, and increased demands facilitated the development of many production centers and defined Sweden's niche in the industry.

Iron and steel have led to the development of a variety of industries that utilize Sweden's metallic resources. These include a significant metal-based power generation industry and a transmission equipment industry. Additionally, numerous small companies producing specialized metal products rely on the iron and steel industry. Sweden also produces a variety of appliances for home and industry, including refrigerators, sewing machines, as well as specialized medical equipment, including dialysis machinery.

Today, 11 steel smelters and 13 mills produce alloy and high-carbon steels, stainless tubing and wire, stainless steel, tool steel, and ordinary steel. Production centers include Ludvika, Gotland, Sandviken, and Hofors. Steel accounts for about 5 percent of Sweden's total exports.

Electric Power

The third major foundation of Sweden's modern economy is electric power. Hydropower first served sawmills and gristmills. In the 1880s, hundreds of small electrical generation stations were added. Once power could be transferred over distances, the government developed large hydropower projects for transportation, industries, and cities.

Sweden developed the turbine, generators, and transmission products needed to maintain and expand the infrastructure of the hydro- and nuclear power industries. These products, needed throughout the world, are produced in Sweden, used in domestic power plants, and exported worldwide.

By 1965, hydropower supplied virtually all of Sweden's electrical needs. Since that time, nuclear power, thermal power, and gas generators have been added to the mix. Today, hydropower and nuclear power each account for 47 percent of the electricity, with the remainder coming from other sources. Sweden is actively researching other energy sources, including wind, solar, and biomass to meet its future energy needs.

Transportation Industry

Sweden has achieved worldwide recognition for manufacturing high-quality automobiles, trucks, buses, locomotives, rolling stock, ships, and aircraft. With a small local market, almost all of this equipment is exported. Historically, two of the major worldwide transportation manufacturers, Volvo and Saab-Scania, were both Swedish companies. In recent years, these companies have split and were purchased by others. Today, Ford Motor Company owns Volvo Cars. The former truck division of Volvo is partly owned by Volkswagen. Recently, Saab-Scania split, and General Motors purchased Saab Automobiles. Swedish investors purchased Scania, which is noted for heavy-duty trucks and buses. Recently, Koenigsegg, a new auto manufacturer, began production of the world's fastest sports car at Ängelholm, in the south.

Defense Industry

Sweden has established a very successful defense products industry. The production of Swedish weapons began with swords in the time of the Vikings. In more recent times, Sweden has produced precision rifles. Currently, its weaponry focus is on defense, although these products may also be used for attack. Sweden's aviation industry formerly produced aircraft, engines, and equipment for both military and civilian use. Now, almost all of its production is for military use.

Communication Technologies

Sweden is also a major player in the world of high technology. The country produces a variety of telecommunications equipment, computer hardware and software, TV and stereos, and communications gear for spacecraft and military use. Ericsson Group, one of the world leaders in cellular phones and wireless technologies, is a major player in this industry.

Sweden has developed an excellent infrastructure for telecommunications. It has more than 6.5 million telephone lines and almost 8 million mobile cellular telephones. That amounts to virtually one cellphone for every person over 7 or 8 years of age! Sweden is home to one AM and 265 FM radio stations and 169 television stations. It ranks among the top nations for Internet access. Almost 57 percent of the people in Sweden have Internet access through 29 Internet service providers.

Cultural Industry

An interesting segment of Sweden's manufacturing economy is its cultural industry. Music, furniture, design, media, advertising, art, and architecture are a few of the components of Swedish cultural influence. At the forefront of this influence is the Swedish music industry that now ranks third in the world. Another Swedish economic and cultural success story is the IKEA Corporation. This large retailer operates stores throughout the world and exports a style and "look" that is uniquely Swedish. Many Swedish designers have enjoyed phenomenal success in the international

IKEA, a retail store that offers a wide range of home furnishings at affordable prices, first opened its doors in Älmhult, Sweden, in 1958. By 2006, there were over 225 stores in 32 countries, including this store in Stockholm.

furniture industry, reflecting the Swedish culture. These are just a few examples of the influence of Swedish culture on the international scene.

SERVICE INDUSTRIES

Two-thirds of Sweden's Gross Domestic Product (GDP) is generated by the service economy. Three of every four of the country's workers are employed in the service industry. Of these, 45 percent are in government jobs in the public sector and 55 percent work with private businesses. Public sector employment includes all people working in governmental agencies, health care, education, homeland security, and social welfare programs. The private sector includes a wide variety of employment, including retail and wholesale trades, tourism and food services, financial services, transportation and communication, real estate, medical care, and a variety of household and business services. These businesses range in size from one or two employees to several thousand workers.

As in manufacturing, the government provides policies and programs for the service industries that facilitate the creation of new business ventures and encourage employment.

Banking and Import-Export Trade

Since 1668, banking in Sweden has operated under the leadership of the Sveriges Riksbank (Bank of Sweden). The Riksbank manages all of Sweden's monetary policies. The basic unit of currency is the Swedish *krona* (SEK). One krona (crown) can be divided into 100 smaller units called *öre*. Coins are based on the öre. The Riksbank is located in Stockholm, as is Sweden's stock exchange.

Sweden has nearly two dozen major commercial banks, along with numerous independent savings banks, and a few partially owned banks. Banking in Sweden is more Internet oriented than in most countries, simply because of the widespread use of business and personal computers. More than a dozen foreign banks operate in the country. These international banks come from the Netherlands, Germany, the United States, and elsewhere and serve the entire Scandinavian region.

The value of Sweden's exports exceeds $120 billion a year. The primary exports include machinery, motor vehicles, pulp and paper products, wood and furniture, iron and steel products, and chemicals. Sweden's major export partners include the United States, Germany, Norway, the United Kingdom, and Denmark. Although the United States is the largest single buyer from Sweden, European Union countries purchase 60 percent of its total exports.

Sweden imports almost $98 billion worth of commodities a year. The major import products are machinery, petroleum, chemicals, vehicles, iron and steel, food products, and clothing. The vast majority of its imports come from European Union nations. Germany alone accounts for one-fifth of the imports. Sweden's exports exceed imports in value by over 24 percent.

Travel and Tourism

Sweden and Denmark are the two most important travel and tourist destinations in Scandinavia. In any given year, one or the other will be the leading destination. The Swedish Travel and Tourism Council promotes tourism worldwide and operates more than 300 local tourist offices to assist visitors. Each year, about 8 million foreign visitors come to Sweden. Travel and tourism contributes more than $10 billion (72 billion SEK), equaling 2.7 percent of the GDP, to the country's economy.

Sweden has established an excellent infrastructure for tourism, including highways, hotels and restaurants, shopping facilities, airports, events, and access to parks. The tourism industry employs more than 320,000 people. These employees are well trained, fluent in many languages, and very welcoming to visitors.

Stockholm, Malmö, and Gothenburg serve as centers for the tourist's arrival and departure. They provide extensive accommodations, visitor sites, events, and activities. Major tourist centers outside these cities are the areas of Dalarna, Värmland, Bohuslän, and Norrbotten. The majority of the visitors to Sweden come from Germany and the neighboring Scandinavian countries.

Sweden offers the visitor beautiful scenery, numerous sightseeing opportunities, bus tours, historic sites, excellent museums, quality shopping, and friendly people. It also offers tourists access to both summer and winter activities, including winter skiing and summer boating and fishing. Sami cultural

Stockholm, Sweden's capital, is one of the most popular tourist destinations in Scandinavia. The city has more than 1,600 restaurants and 3,600 stores, and is home to the greatest concentration of art galleries and museums in the world.

areas are becoming increasingly popular visitor sites. Foreign visitors of Swedish heritage are increasingly important to the tourist trade as they seek information about their ancestral homeland and long-lost relatives.

Transportation and Communication

Despite its size and shape, Sweden's transportation infrastructure is excellent and continually improving. Historically, the need to move minerals, wood, and manufactured products to consumer markets benefited transportation. These industries brought about the development of railroads, highways, and port facilities in the country.

About 79 percent of Sweden's 132 highways (totaling 479 miles, or 770 kilometers) are paved. The forest areas possess an almost equal mileage of private unpaved roads. Sweden has 700 miles (1,126 kilometers) of modern motorways. Most of the travel in Sweden is by private automobile, buses, or railroads. In some of the more isolated rural areas access is by automobile or truck only.

Railroads in Sweden operate on standard-gauge track. A total of 7,072 miles (11,481 kilometers) of track are operational in the country. Of that total, over 45 percent is electrified, and most of Sweden's railroad engines are electric. The government-owned track connects mining and forest areas with ports and also links cities and scenic areas.

Three major airports in Sweden dominate air travel. They are: Arlanda in Stockholm, Landvetter in Gothenburg, and Sturup at Malmö. Major air carriers include SAS, Lufthansa, British Airways, and Finnair.

Water transportation is also important to Sweden. The major port cities of Gavle, Göteborg, Halmstad, Helsingborg, and Hudiksvall host shipping from around the world. The Göta Canal provides inland water travel connecting Gothenburg and Stockholm. Today, the canal is utilized primarily for pleasure craft and tourist boats. Car ferries connect Sweden with neighboring countries and the United Kingdom. In 2005, the kings of Norway and Sweden dedicated the Svinesund Bridge, a spectacular span over the Oresund Straight that connects Sweden and Denmark by rail and road. This world's largest single-arched bridge joins these two countries just south of Oslo.

SUMMARY

Sweden has a superb manufacturing and service economy. It has effectively utilized its traditional economic activities as the basis for a diverse and vibrant modern economy based on manufacturing and services. The government, through taxation and legislation, is deeply involved in both the traditional and the modern industrialized economies. The diversified traditional economy built on agriculture, forestry, and minerals is strong and has benefited from many supportive government programs. The modern industrialized economy, based on steel, hydroelectric power, transportation, and communication technologies, produces high-quality products. Sweden's unique collaboration of economics and government has supported the production of quality products and services that are in demand worldwide. The result of this unique combination of economies and government is a worldwide demand for Sweden's many quality products and services and a strong vibrant economy for the people of Sweden.

CHAPTER

7

Living in Sweden

The Julbord (Yule table) is a simplified version of the smorgasbord. Unlike traditional multicourse Swedish smorgasbord, the Christmas Julbord consists of only four courses. Tradition requires that both the Julbord and the smorgasbord begin each course with a clean plate. The first course of cold fish dishes includes herring, salmon, eel, and other seafoods. The second course of thinly sliced cold meats includes julskina (Christmas ham), roast beef, and turkey. The third course includes traditional hot dishes plus stuffed cabbage rolls, pickled pigs' feet, pork ribs, and lutfisk (dried cod). The fourth course is the optional dessert selection that includes rice porridge, pies, and pastries. Traditional vegetables, breads, and condiments are included with each course.

The Julbord is a feast that incorporates all the cultural traditions, beliefs, and values of the Swedish people. This holiday season is so important that it is celebrated from St. Lucia's Day on December 13

In Sweden, the Christmas holiday season lasts from December 13 (St. Lucia's Day) through January 6 (Twelfth Night). Pictured here are kindergarten students dressed as Santa Claus and Santa Lucia at a celebration of St. Lucia's Day.

through the Twelfth Night, on January 6. The traditions, beliefs, and values celebrated during this season are the essential elements underpinning everyday life in Sweden.

The Swedish educational system strives to provide equal opportunity to all, while providing students with an appreciation of Swedish history and values. These values are reinforced across the curriculum in courses such as literature, film, music, dance, architecture, the fine arts, and sport. Swedish society protects from cradle to grave and also nurtures cultural appreciation and preservation.

LANGUAGE

Swedish is the language most spoken, although minority languages are respected. As early as 200 A.D., Viking peoples developed a written runic alphabet containing 24 letters. This alphabet, combined with carved pictures, enabled them to communicate their history, record epic events, and conduct business.

Following the end of Viking dominance in the 1100s, Old Norse (North Germanic) became the primary language of Scandinavia. Today, Swedish, Norwegian, Icelandic, and Danish languages are similar because they are all related to Old Norse. If you are fluent in one of these languages, you will understand the others. Sweden does not have an official language, but Swedish is the dominant tongue. Because both English and Swedish are taught in school, most Swedes are fluent in both languages. Further, the use of the Internet has increased the number of English words used in Swedish daily life.

Many minority languages are spoken in Sweden, with Finnish and Sami being the most prominent. Meänkieli-Finnish Sami, Romany, and Jiddisch are also officially recognized minority languages. Additionally, there is an increased usage of immigrant languages. More than 100,000 of the immigrant people speak Arabic or Persian as their primary language.

RELIGION

For more than 500 years, the Swedish Evangelical Lutheran Church has been the dominant religion. Although most Swedes claim Church membership, Sweden is considered a secular country.

Religion in Sweden has changed significantly over time. The Vikings worshiped several gods, including Wodan (Odin), Tor (Thor), Frej (Frö), and the goddess Frevia (Freyja). These gods lived in Valhalla (Viking heaven) with deceased heroic Viking warriors.

In 829 A.D., Ansgar, a Benedictine monk, introduced Christianity to Sweden. King Olof Skötkonung was the first ruler to convert to Christianity, about 200 years later. In 1164, the pope established a Roman Catholic archdiocese at Uppsala. In 1210, church and state were united when Erik Knutson ruled as king and bishop. The Roman Catholic Church was the dominant faith until 1523. In that year, King Gustav I Vasa broke from Rome and established the Swedish Evangelical Lutheran Church as the state religion.

After the Protestant Reformation, babies born in Sweden between 1523 and 1996 were baptized in the state church. In 1996, this requirement was lifted, and in 2000, Sweden officially separated church and state. Although 87 percent of the people belong to the Swedish Evangelical Lutheran Church, only 10 percent regularly attend services.

Because most Swedes do not actively participate in religion, the country is considered one of the most secular nations in Europe. Some residents, often immigrants, do attend church regularly. Roman Catholicism, various Protestant and Orthodox faiths, Islam, Buddhism, and Judaism are all practiced in Sweden. The major religious holidays are celebrated by both those who profess religion and those who do not.

EDUCATION

Equal access to free public education is a basic tenet of Swedish life. All children aged 7 to 16 years are required to attend school. Publicly funded preschools and day care are now part of Sweden's education system, and most preschoolers participate in these programs. Monthly government allowances help families support each child.

Students normally enter Sweden's compulsory school system at 7 years of age. Nine years of free, compulsory schooling consists of three levels—lower, middle, and upper. The lower equates to our primary grades 1–3, middle to grades 4–6, and upper compulsory compares to grades 7–9. Compulsory school curriculum is standardized for all children 7–13 years, with some elective curriculum in the upper level.

Upper Secondary school is free, and attendance optional. Ninety-eight percent of the compulsory school graduates do attend Upper Secondary school (U.S. grades 10–12). The Upper Secondary curriculum requires that all students complete eight core subjects: Swedish or Swedish as a second language, English, mathematics, science, social science, religious studies, sport and health, and art.

Public higher education is also free. Universities, colleges, and technical schools are located throughout Sweden to facilitate universal access. There are 13 public universities, with 23 colleges offering undergraduate degrees, plus colleges of health science and technical institutes. Sweden's prestigious University of Uppsala is more than 500 years old.

Sweden's commitment to universal education is reflected in its student enrollment. Approximately one million students attend Compulsory school, with another 300,000 in Upper Secondary school. An additional 300,000 students are enrolled in universities, colleges, and technical institutes. More than 350,000 people are enrolled in adult education programs. These programs include Sfi (Swedish for immigrants), designed to provide newly arrived citizens basic knowledge of Swedish language and history.

Private schools are present at all educational levels. Although few in number, they are most popular at the preschool and day-care levels. Private education must meet the same requirements established for public schools. About 3 percent of the students attend private schools.

Contemporary Sweden is recognized as a world-renowned center for literature. The National Agency for Education supervises the educational system. With recent reforms, local municipalities have become increasingly responsible for compulsory and upper-level schools. National and local governments work closely with parents and teachers to meet individual special needs.

LITERATURE

Sweden is home to seven Nobel Laureates: Selma Lagerlöf, Verner von Heidenstam, Erik Axel Karlfeldt, Pär Lagerkvist, Nelly Sachs, Eyvind Johnson, and Harry Martinson. Popular contemporary Swedish author Astrid Lindgren gained international fame as the creator of the Pippi Longstocking books. Her works, featuring the young heroine Pippi Longstocking, have won numerous awards, including the Rabén & Sjögren's Best Children's Book prize, the Hans Christian Andersen Award, and the UNESCO International Book Award. Her home community of Vimmerby has established Astrid Lindgren's World and Gardens as a children's theme park and center.

FILM

Sweden's film industry is noted for producing quality films enjoyed locally, regionally, and worldwide. Swedish films reflect themes of nature, intimacy, psychology, spirituality, literature, dreams, and, of course, Pippi Longstocking. Many of Sweden's movie directors and actors have achieved worldwide recognition. Victor Sjöström, Lasse Hallström, and Oscar winner Ernst Ingmar Bergman are among directors of note. Greta Garbo, Ingrid Bergman, and Peter Stormare are a few of Sweden's world-famous movie stars.

MUSIC AND DANCE

Music and dance play important roles in Swedish nationalism, tourism, and festivals. *Folkmusik* (traditional music) and

Swedes often dress in folk costume and dance to traditional music (folkmusik) during festivals. Sweden is renowned for its folk music, which includes polka, schottis, waltz, polska, and mazurka.

folkdance remain important in contemporary Sweden. During Midsummer's Day, a notable music festival, the citizenry dance and sing as they ring the flower-adorned maypole.

Of the numerous music festivals held each year, the Hultsfred Festival in Småland is considered the most important. The festivals feature traditional instruments and dance that follows the sounds and rhythms of the music. Polska music is the most popular and the fiddle is the most common instrument. Tradition holds that fiddlers learned to play the instrument from Nacken, a music-playing, river-dwelling water spirit. Other traditional instruments include the accordion, key fiddle, recorder, flute, and Swedish bagpipe.

The Swedish people strongly support symphonies, opera, choirs, festivals, jazz, and rock/pop music. Virtually every county has a symphonic or chamber orchestra. Swedish opera has produced the world famous singers Jenny Lind, Christina Nilsson, and Birgit Nilsson. Religious or secular choirs generally perform at all cultural and social activities. Contemporary jazz, pop, and rock music are popular elements of urban nightlife. Sweden is behind only the United States and Great Britain in influencing contemporary music. Noted performers of the "Swedish commercial sound" include ABBA, Roxette, the Cardigans, Ace of Base, and Dr. Alban.

ARCHITECTURE AND DESIGN

For hundreds of years, wood was Sweden's most important building material. Wooden structures dotted the landscape. During the early part of the twentieth century, magnificent wooden homes were built in many cities. Today, wooden homes are most popular as summer homes. In Sweden's urban areas, stone, brick, and other building materials have been used for homes, apartments, and other urban buildings.

In the twentieth century, Sweden emerged as a worldwide major architectural and design center. Early in the century, city planners incorporated open spaces into urban design and growth. Stockholm's City Hall, designed by Ragnar Östberg, and built in the early 1900s, is famous for its urban classicism. Swedish architecture was further inspired by early 1900 social reforms that used standardization as a way to improve housing for all. The standardized kitchen designs of Osvald Almqvist are early examples of Swedish functionalism.

Gunnar Asplund was the principal architect of the 1930 Stockholm exhibition that embraced Swedish Functionalism. Asplund, along with city planner Sven Markelius, architect/ social functionalist Uno Åhrén, and furniture designers Carl Larsson and Bruno Mathsson were instrumental in establishing Swedish functionalism.

Today, Swedish functionalism design is simple, functional and sparse, and planned; emphasizes clean lines; and pays homage to nature. IKEA, an international Swedish furniture store, provides an excellent example of Swedish functionalism. The design of the stores and the furniture sold within reflect contemporary Swedish architecture and design.

An exciting addition to Sweden's architectural landscape is located in Malmö. In 2005, the "Turning Torso," Scandinavia's tallest building, was completed. Its uniquely designed twisting framework offers testament to Sweden's continued leadership in architecture and design.

ART AND ARTIFACTS

Sweden is home to numerous museums. Its cultural heritage lives in its preserved castles and palaces, carvings in rock and wood, stave churches, farmsteads, parks, museums, and heritage centers. Among the most prominent of Sweden's 350 museums are the Nationalmuseum (antiquities), the Vasa Museum (a 1620s warship and other seventeenth-century artifacts), the Royal Palace, and Skansen (cultural heritage park), all located in Stockholm.

Swedish artisans are quite eclectic. Folk art is commonly reflected in brightly colored, handcrafted objects, especially the famous Dala horse, a favorite of tourists. It is also reflected in glass and crystal items sold to tourists and world markets. For more than 100 years, Swedish artists, including Bruno Liljefors and Anders Zorn, have focused on nature. More recently, artists such as Annika von Hausswolff and Annika Eriksson have gained international reputations. The fantastic works of the sculptor Carl Milles are displayed at Millesgården. Numerous examples of Milles' work are can be seen in public spaces and museums in America.

Two recent additions to the art scene have enhanced Sweden's role in the art world. The first, the Moderna Museet, is widely recognized as a major international trendsetter among modern museums. Second, Stockholm's subway system provides an unusual venue. Artists display their work throughout the subway system, which has become the world's longest art gallery.

SPORTS

The Swedish people love outdoor recreation and sports. More than one-half of the people belong to a fitness center, recreation center, or sports club. The Swedish motto "sports for all" has produced a land of many athletes.

Skiing and ice-skating are both popular during Sweden's long winter. Sweden's oldest sport is cross-country skiing, which originated, not as a sport, but as a form of winter transportation. Alpine skiing that includes both downhill and ski jumping is popular in the northern regions. Ice skaters enjoy using the thousands of lakes throughout Sweden for pleasure skating, speed skating, and figure skating. Skaters also thrive on games of hockey and bandy (using a ball rather than a puck). Competitions in both cross-country skiing and long-distance skating are popular winter events.

During the summer, popular sports and activities are also enjoyed outdoors. Families and individuals enjoy walking, jogging, hiking, and biking. The sport of orienteering, which originated in Sweden, is a popular cross-country activity. With Sweden's 100,000 lakes and the sea, water sports and activities are extremely popular. Fishing, swimming, sailing, and boating are important water activities. Tennis and badminton are also played in Sweden, and golf has been growing in popularity. With the midnight sun, during the summer golfers can tee-off at any time of day or night.

Football (soccer) is played and followed avidly by fans throughout the country. When the Swedish National Team competes in the World Cup, all of Sweden follows the games closely. Most Europeans love to watch the World Cup tournament each year and take great pride in their country's team.

Some of Sweden's more notable sport stars include Björn Borg (tennis), Ingemar Stenmark (alpine skiing), Gunde

Svan (cross-country skiing), Annika Sörenstam (golf), Niklas Lidström (ice hockey), Fredrik Ljungberg (soccer), Kajsa Bergqvist and Gunder Hagg (track and field), and Ingemar Johansson (boxing).

GENEALOGY

Genealogy is becoming increasingly important in Sweden. The 2000 U.S. Census lists almost 4 million Americans of Swedish ancestry. Many of them travel to Sweden to research their family background. Others hire researchers to find information about homelands, ancestors, and current Swedish relatives.

Since Swedish immigration is relatively recent, it is often possible to obtain oral and written information about one's ancestors or homelands. For individuals seeking genealogical information, Sweden offers access to a variety of services and resources, including church, birth, death, probate, census, land ownership, and tax records. With successful research, many Swedish Americans are able to visit the original family farm or village and sometimes locate living family members along the way.

SUMMARY

The Swedish people enjoy a high standard of living. They share a common language as well as a statewide church, although few attend church services. Swedes value their heritage and celebrate the national holidays, which are often based on religious festivities. Sweden has established a premier public school system, accessible to all. People enjoy and participate in activities related to Swedish literature, film, music, dance, arts, design, and architecture. The Swedish people today are well educated, are provided many services by the state, and enjoy a life rich in recreational and cultural opportunities.

8

Sweden Looks Ahead

Each chapter of this geography of Sweden has started with a
dinner course from a Swedish smorgasbord. We hope these
introductions have helped you understand the importance of
this feast in Swedish households. By now, you should be full, but if
you still have room for more, why not try a Swedish Fish? This
delightful red candy tastes like a very flavorful Gummy Bear.

Similarly, each chapter has examined one aspect of Sweden's
diverse geographic conditions. Like dishes in a smorgasbord, these
chapters help us to taste and savor the various characteristics of
Sweden's geography. Our hope is to provide you with an appreciation
of this geographic smorgasbord. You have explored and experienced
the physical environment of this beautiful land. You have also
examined the cultural heritage of the people and studied the major
social, economic, and governmental elements that provide you with
an intellectual understanding of contemporary Sweden.

We began our journey of geography with an analysis of Sweden's physical geography. Sweden has a diverse glaciated landscape composed of mountains, hills, and interior and coastal plains. Its coastal areas are complex and include fjords, fjards, and numerous islands.

Three different climate zones exist in Sweden. The extreme southern area has a Marine West Coast climate. The central and northern zones each cover about 40 percent of the country. The central zone is home to the Humid Continental Long Winter climate, whereas the northern zone is dominated by the Polar Tundra climate.

Sixty percent of Sweden is covered by spruce and pine forests. The Norway spruce is the dominant tree type. Mixed forests that include pine, spruce, birch, and aspen are found in the southern third of Sweden. Reindeer, moose, deer, and other animals inhabit the land. Sweden is also home to a variety of birds and many forms of sea life.

Sweden's first human occupants arrived from Central Asia about 10,000 years ago. They are believed to have been ancient ancestors of the Sami. Germanic peoples from the south occupied southern Sweden during the Stone Age, Bronze Age, and Iron Age. Evidence of these early inhabitants can be seen today in the presence of cairns, burial mounds, and stone ships. Artifacts from this era are also on display in Sweden's numerous museums.

Beginning in the eighth century, the Vikings expanded beyond Scandinavia. Swedish Vikings gained control over neighboring Baltic Sea areas and extended their control into Russia and the Ukraine. Viking warriors went to sea to gain access to the wealth of other lands. Some treasures were taken in battle, but others were acquired through skillful trading. The Vikings established forts and settlements. In some areas they occupied the land. In Russia and the Ukraine, their intermarriage with the Slavs was the beginning of today's Russian people. The Vikings were likely the most powerful people of their time.

Following the Viking Age, which ended between 1040 and 1100 A.D., Sweden went though a series of struggles as monarch and assemblies vied for power. The Kalmar Union, which unified Sweden, Denmark, and Norway, proved unsuccessful. Not until 1521 A.D., when Gustav I Vasa became king, did Sweden emerge from these struggles. The years from 1611 to 1721 A.D. are considered Sweden's Age of Greatness. During this time, Sweden established an empire that included parts of Norway, Sweden, Russia, Latvia, Estonia, Germany, and the Netherlands. This era ended with constitutional changes that weakened the monarchy and increased the power of the parliament.

In 1814, following the Napoleonic Wars, Sweden obtained control of Norway. Their union lasted until 1905 when Norway was able to successfully and peacefully gain its independence. The last 100 years have seen Sweden evolve into the world's premier welfare state. The Swedish System provides "cradle to grave" care for all of Sweden's residents. It is a governmental model that requires high taxes and extensive governmental controls. This system works well for the Swedish people, who take pride in and are protective of their government. Today, Sweden is a member of the European Union, which is helping to shape the future of Europe.

Sweden is a land of 9 million people. Its population distribution corresponds with its physical geography and its urban development. The indigenous Sami occupy the cold northern landscape. The vast forests are sparsely populated, except for major milling and mining areas. Coastal communities and southern agricultural areas are the most densely populated, with 84 percent of the people living in urban areas.

Sweden experienced extensive immigration to the United States from 1820 to 1960. During that time more than 1.3 million people left for America. They migrated to the rich agricultural American Midwest. More recently, Swedish immigrants have moved to New England and the Pacific Northwest. Today, Sweden is experiencing substantial immigration. Immigrants

Carl XVI Gustaf, who has served as Sweden's king since 1973, is pictured here receiving flowers from Swedish children during his 59th birthday celebration in April 2005 at the courtyard of the Royal Palace in Stockholm. Although the king's duties are largely ceremonial, he is an important part of Sweden's heritage.

primarily come from European countries, but more recently people from the Middle East, South Asia, East Asia, and Africa are seeking new lives in Sweden. Sweden, like neighboring Norway, is committed to assuring Sami people the same rights afforded all Swedish citizens.

The Kingdom of Sweden is a constitutional monarchy. Since 1719, the Riksdag has enacted legislation for Sweden. Today, the king plays a ceremonial role in the Swedish government. Most of the power is now in the unicameral Riksdag and its appointed prime minister.

Sweden's commitment to social welfare programming and protections plays a vital role in the life of every citizen. The government is involved in furthering and protecting Sweden's economy. The economy generates the tax income required to support the social welfare programs. Combined industrialization and social welfare programs have resulted in an impressive standard of living for the people. As it does today, Sweden, in the future, will likely strive to maintain a standard of living that preserves and enhances the social welfare of its people.

Facts at a Glance

Name	Kingdom of Sweden
Background	A military power in the seventeenth century. For the last two centuries, Sweden has avoided participation in any war. It even preserved armed neutrality during World War II. Sweden today is a long-successful capitalistic nation with a representative democracy, ceremonial monarchy, and significant welfare system. Sweden delayed entering the European Union until 1995 and waived the adoption of the euro in 1999.
Relative Location	In Northern Europe, bordering the Baltic Sea, Gulf of Bothnia, Kattegat, and Skagerrak, and situated between Norway (north and west), Denmark (south), and Finland (north and east)
Absolute Location	62 degrees north latitude, 15 degrees east longitude
Area	173,732 square miles (449,964 square kilometers); slightly smaller than Iowa, Missouri, and Arkansas combined
Coastline	2,000 miles (3,218 kilometers)
Climate	A cold land tempered by the Gulf Stream. Temperate in south with cold, cloudy winters and cool partly cloudy summers. Subarctic in north; midnight sun in the north
Terrain	Flat to gently rolling lowlands, with mountains in the west
Elevations	Lowest point: Lake Hammarsjon (reclaimed bay near Kristianstad),−7.90 feet (−2.41 meters). Highest point: Mt. Kebnekaise, 6,926 feet (2,111 meters)
Minerals	Iron ore, copper, lead, zinc, gold, silver, tungsten, uranium, arsenic, feldspar
Population	9,001,774 (2005 est.)
Religions	87 percent Evangelical Lutheran Church of Sweden. Others: Roman Catholic, Orthodox, Baptist, Muslim, Jewish, Buddhist.
Languages	Swedish, with small minorities of Sami- and Finnish-speaking peoples.
Literacy	99 percent of the population
Government	Constitutional monarchy

Capital	Stockholm
Counties	21 counties (*lan,* singular and plural): Blekinge, Dalarnas, Gavleborgs, Gotlands, Hallands, Jämtlands, Jonkopings, Kalmar, Kronobergs, Norrbottens, Örebro, Ostergotlands, Skåne, Sodermanlands, Stockholms, Uppsala, Varmlands, Vasterbottens, Vasternorrlands, Vastmanlands, and Vastra Gotalands
Independence Day	Nationaldag (National Day), June 6. On this date in 1523, Gustav Vasa was elected king.
National Holiday	June 6, Flag Day
Agriculture Products	Barley, wheat, sugar beets, meat, milk
Industries	Iron and steel, precision equipment (bearings, communication technologies, defense industries, chemicals, wood pulp and paper products, processed foods, automobiles and trucks)
Exports	Machinery, motor vehicles, paper products, pulp and wood, iron and steel products, chemicals
Imports	Machinery, petroleum and petroleum products, chemicals, motor vehicles, iron and steel, foodstuffs, clothing
Currency	Swedish krona (SEK)
Railways	7,072 miles (11,481 kilometers) of standard-gauge track; 5,840 miles (9,400 kilometers) of electrified track (2004)
Highways	132,499 miles (213,237 kilometers) total; 104,144 miles (167,604 kilometers) paved (includes 958 miles or 1,542 kilometers of expressways); 28,355 miles (45,633 kilometers) unpaved (2002)
Airports	Stockholm (Arlanda), Gothenburg, Landvetter, and Sturup
Other Surface Links	Bridge over Oresund Strait to Denmark; car/bus ferries to Denmark, Norway, Finland, Baltic States, and Great Britain
Major Ports	Gavle, Goteborg, Halmstad, Helsingborg, Hudiksvall, Kalmar, Karlshamn, Lulea, Malmo, Solvesborg, Stockholm, Sundsvall.

History at a Glance

12,000 B.C.	Ice Age ends. Landscape is again visible; plant life blossoms.
8,000	First human occupants appear on the Swedish landscape.
5,000	Germanic agriculturalists arrive in Sweden.
1,800	Bronze Age people arrive in Sweden.
500	Iron Age reaches Sweden from Germanic south. People live in relative isolation for the next 1,000 years.
A.D. 700	Viking Age begins.
793	Vikings attack London.
800s	Vikings cross Baltic Sea and establish control over Finland, Estonia, Latvia, Lithuania, Russia, Belarus, and Ukraine.
829	German monk Ansgar introduces Christianity to Sweden.
840	Vikings establish city of Dublin on island of Ireland.
862	Viking Chieftain Rurik becomes ruler of the Slavs.
912	Igor establishes Rurik Dynasty, which ruled Russia until 1598.
1001	Leif Eriksson reaches Vinland (North America).
1069	End of the Viking Age in Sweden.
1397	Under the leadership of Queen Margrethe, Union of Kalmar unites Demark, Norway, and Sweden.
1523	Gustav I Vasa drives Danes from Sweden, becomes king, and establishes the Evangelical Lutheran Church as the Church of Sweden.
1611	The Age of Greatness begins as Sweden becomes the most powerful nation in northern Europe.
1719	Sweden enacts new constitution that transfers governmental control from the monarch to the Riksdag.
1810	French Prince Jean Baptiste Jules Bernadotte, becomes King Charles XIV John, and establishes Bernadotte monarchy, which continues today.
1814	Napoleon defeated by British. Norway placed under control of Sweden. Union of Sweden and Norway begins.
1818	Union of Sweden and Norway becomes a neutral nation. Great migration from Sweden to America begins.
1905	National referendum in Norway leads to independence from Sweden.

1929 Worldwide Great Depression ensues, and Hitler's power emerges in Germany.

1940 Norway falls to German forces despite its neutrality. Sweden sustains its neutrality but is forced to allow the German Army to cross its territory.

1946 Sweden joins the United Nations.

1953 Dag Hammarskjöld becomes Secretary General of the United Nations.

1995 Sweden joins the European Union.

Further Reading

Bankston, John. *Alfred Nobel and the Story of the Nobel Prize.* Hockessin, DE: Mitchell Lane, 2004.

Hudson, Strode. *Of Swedish Ways.* Minneapolis, MN: Dillon Press, 1971.

Mead, W.R., *An Historical Geography of Scandinavia.* New York: Academic Press, 1981.

Miles, Lee, ed. *Sweden and the European Union.* London: Continuum International, 2001.

Nordstrom, Byron J. *The History of Sweden.* Westport, CT: Greenwood Press, 2002.

O'Dell, Andrew C. *The Scandinavian World.* London: Longmans, 1963.

Ostergren, Robert C., and John G. Rice. *The Europeans: A Geography of People, Culture, and Environment.* New York: Guilford, 2004.

Scott, Franklin D. *Sweden: The Nation's History.* Carbondale, IL: Southern Illinois University Press, 1989.

Somme, Axel. *A Geography of Norden.* London: Heinemann, 1968.

Streiffert, Bo, ed. *Sweden.* Eyewitness Travel Guides. New York: DK Publishing, 2005.

Wastenson, Leif, ed. *National Atlas of Sweden.* 19 Volumes. Stockholm: Almqvist & Wiksell, 1990 to present.

Widenheim, Cecilia, ed. *Utopia and Reality: Modernity in Sweden, 1900–1960.* New Haven, CT: Yale University Press, 2002.

CIA—The World Factbook, Sweden
http://www.cia.gov/cia/publications/factbook/geos/sw.html

Languages of Sweden
http://www.ethnologue.com/show_country.asp?name=Sweden

The Swedish Presidency: Geography
http://www.eu2001.se/static/eng/facts/kort_geografi.asp

Sweden: External Trade
http://www.link2exports.co.uk/regions.asp?lsid=1968&pid=1467

Travel to Sweden
http://www.northerner.com/sweden.html

Swedish Parliament
http://www.riksdagen.se/index_en.asp

Demographic Statistics of Sweden
http://www.scb.se/default____2154.asp

A Brief Survey of Tornadoes in Sweden
http://www.svemet.org/tornado.html

Swedish Institute: How Is the Swedish Model Faring?
http://sweden.se/templates/cs/Article____2891.aspx

The Official Gateway to Sweden
http://www.sweden.se

Sweden and the Swedes
http://www.sweden.se/templates/cs/SASLauncher____2384.aspx?topicID=2027

The Dynamics of Immigrant Welfare and Labor Market Behavior
http://www.utdallas.edu/~lofstrom/Welfaredynamics.pdf

Swedish Travel and Tourism Council
http://www.visit-sweden.com/VSTemplates/MarketStartPage____7360.aspx

Index

Index

Index

About the Contributors

EDWARD PATRICK HOGAN is Professor Emeritus of Geography at South Dakota State University and the State Geographer of South Dakota. In addition to his career teaching geography, Ed is Associate Vice President Emeritus for Academic Affairs and Chief Information Technology Officer Emeritus for South Dakota State University. Ed and his daughter Erin Hogan Fouberg have coauthored *Norway* (Chelsea House, 2004), *Ireland* (Chelsea House, 2003), and *The Geography of South Dakota* (Center for Western Studies, 2001). Ed has authored numerous articles, television series, and publications related to types of housing around the world, migration, economic development, and regional geography. He received the Distinguished Teaching Award from the National Council for Geographic Education and in 1992 was included in the book *Leaders in American Geography* as one of 79 people who have most influenced geographic education in the United States. He especially enjoys being with his family, listening to traditional Irish music, and creating works of art.

JOAN MARIE HOGAN is the producer and co-host of *Homespun Medicine*, a weekly local call-in radio talk show. Joan also produces and co-hosts *Homespun Medical Tips*, a three-minute radio program that airs weekly on radio stations throughout the state of South Dakota. The program features physicians from across the state discussing their special medical interests. Both radio programs inform listeners in an entertaining manner about their medical health. Joan has been an Instructor in Communication Studies and Theatre at South Dakota State University. Joan and her husband, Ed, have made numerous trips to Europe over the last ten years. In 2002, they developed a unique tour of Ireland, *Sacred Sites and Irish Nights*, which they direct yearly with the 1 2 Travel Company of County Cork. Joan has been a board member of the Brookings Chamber of Commerce Board of Directors as well as a board member of the South Dakota Board of Pharmacy. Joan enjoys time spent with family, especially her grandchildren.

CHARLES F. "FRITZ" GRITZNER is Distinguished Professor of Geography at South Dakota University in Brookings. He is now in his fifth decade of college teaching and research. During his career, he has taught more than 60 different courses, spanning the fields of physical, cultural, and regional geography. In addition to his teaching, he enjoys writing, working with teachers, and sharing his love for geography with students. As consulting editor for the MODERN WORLD NATIONS series, he has a wonderful opportunity to combine each of these "hobbies." Fritz has served as both President and Executive Director of the National Council for Geographic Education and has received the Council's highest honor, the George J. Miller Award for Distinguished Service. In March 2004, he won the Distinguished Teaching award from the Association of American Geographers at their annual meeting held in Philadelphia.